W.C. FIELDS

A Pyramid Illustrated History of the Movies

by
NICHOLAS YANNI

General Editor: TED SENNETT

PYRAMID
PUBLICATIONS
NEW YORK

For my Mother and Father,
who were born and raised, married and authored me in Philadelphia,
the city that W.C. Fields loved to hate (thus proving it can't be all bad).

W.C. FIELDS
A Pyramid Illustrated History of the Movies

Copyright © 1974 by Pyramid Communications, Inc.

First edition published October, 1974

Second printing, October 1975

ISBN 0-515-03486-X

Library of Congress Catalog Card Number: 74-1591

Printed in the United States of America

Pyramid Books are published by Pyramid Communications, Inc. Its trademarks, consisting of the word "Pyramid" and the portrayal of a pyramid, are registered in the United States Patent Office.

Pyramid Communications, Inc.
919 Third Avenue, New York, N.Y. 10022

(graphic design by anthony basile)

ACKNOWLEDGMENTS

I would like to express my appreciation to the following people for their kindness in assisting me during the research and preparation of this book: Patrick Sheehan and the motion picture collection of the Library of Congress; the staff of the Theatre Collection, New York Public Library at Lincoln Center; Charles Silver at the Museum of Modern Art Film Study Center; The Echo Book Shop; William K. Everson and Adam Reilly for so generously making their Fields films available to me; and, of course, Ted Sennett for his advice and encouragement during the writing of this book.

Photographs: Jerry Vermilye, The Museum of Modern Art—Stills Collection, Movie Star News, Cinemabilia and United Press International.

CONTENTS

T. Frothingwell Bellows. Egbert Sousé. Larson E. Whipsnade. Eustace McGargle. What do these gentlemen all have in common besides an outrageous name, a braying, raucous, nasally tinny voice, and a large, bulbous nose? They are all the creations of William Claude Dukenfield, otherwise known as W.C. Fields, a master of comedy who remains, nearly thirty years after his death, a legendary figure for a new generation of filmgoers, an endearing memory for those who remember his movies, and a continual source of uproarious laughter.

W.C. Fields delighted in debunking myths—*all* myths—and he would probably be a bit mystified and even suspicious of some of the legends that have developed around him today. He would also be surprised that filmgoers could feel benign toward a man who was so savage about their foibles and their pious attitudes. Various biographers have chronicled his alleged meanness, penchant for fraud, arrogance, addiction to alcohol, on-again, off-again cruelty, callousness toward friends, women, clergy, children, dogs, and others. He was *not* lovable. Yet today's filmgoers might also understand this basic fact about Fields: he was merely playing straight man to a malevolent universe which he probably (and rightfully so) believed had singled him

INTRODUCTION: THE FIELDSIAN STYLE

out for destruction.

Most of his life had been spent trying to exact vengeance against (or simply thumbing his nose at) this hostile universe. In fact, many of his admirers and critics believe that his later personal and professional life was dedicated to repaying society for the hurts of his childhood. But his adult life also produced "enemies": doctors, lawyers, grasping women, noisome, bratty children, and even inanimate objects, such as cars and golf clubs. Wherever he turned, it seemed that some force, human or otherwise, was trying to wrest control of his life.

Inevitably, this angered and demoralized him, and affected his work. In life and on screen and stage, Fields was at his greatest only when he was able to take full control of the situation. In his later years, with Universal, he was allowed this luxury—and it showed in the brilliant, freewheeling last four feature films in which he starred. With Paramount, the other major studio for which he worked, his power was not always complete—but even there, such films as *You're Telling Me*, *It's a Gift*, and *Man on the Flying Trapeze* contain indestructi-

11

ble gems of comic art imbedded in their often ramshackle structure.

Director Gregory La Cava, who first met Fields when they made two silents on Long Island in 1927-28 (*So's Your Old Man* and *Running Wild*) and with whom Fields would become a life-long friend, said of him: "Nearly everything Bill tried to get into his movies was something that lashed out at the world. The peculiar thing is that although he was being pretty mean, there wasn't any real sting in it. It was only funny. Bill never really wanted to hurt anybody. He just felt an obligation."

It is said that from his deathbed on Christmas Day in 1946 he recited long passages from Dickens, particularly the character of Mr. Micawber, the role he played in *David Copperfield* (1935) for MGM. This is fitting, for both on screen (where he wanted to be thought of as essentially a con-man) and off-screen (where he often *was*), Fields amply demonstrated that art imitates life. For although he was no Micawber in voice, appearance or manners, somehow Fields contrived to suggest that character's indomitable romanticism and spirit. As British critic, Kenneth Tynan, has remarked: "Always his face looked injured. Fields, quiescent and smoldering, is funnier than Fields rampant and yelling."*

Today's audiences remember the raffish cadence of Fields' nasal drawl and his fleshy-nosed charlatan manner, the small wars he fought against a seemingly hostile world, and the precise manner in which he always drew a deadly bead on most middle-class values. When Fields says "It was a woman that drove me to drink—and I never even had the decency to write and thank her," we know he meant it with all his heart. This likable villain and conniving charlatan had a wicked, prickly sense of humor—and he almost always made sure we felt it.

Tynan sums it all up in this way: "Fields admits a line, rather than speaks it. His nose resembles a doughnut pickled in vinegar or an eroded squash ball."** This is a bit harsh, and Fields would surely have taken umbrage at the pointed remark about his nose (he was most sensitive about that subject), but it is essentially an accurate characterization of the man's unique presence.

*Kenneth Tynan, *Curtains* (New York: Atheneum, 1961), p. 355
**Ibid., p. 356.

So much has already been said about the early years of W.C. Fields that the story has almost taken on the legendary quality of a chapter from a Dickens novel or *Huckleberry Finn*. Fields was born in West Philadelphia, in the early part of 1880 to Englishman James Dukenfield and Kate Felton, a neighbor's daughter. Fields, named William Claude, ran away from home at age eleven when, as the story goes, he became angered when his father hit him on the head with a shovel.

Young Fields thought his father's act an injustice—and, being independent-minded, sensitive but with a touch of bravura, he mulled over the situation. Several days later, he hit his father on the head from above with a large wooden box and then ran out of the house, never to return as a child. Thus, young Fields may owe his entire career to his father's providing him with the right incentive to get out into the world. On his own, and of a determined mind, he escaped the usual regimentation a child receives in school.

Before this incident, however, Fields had worked with his father, a vegetable seller, and had learned to read and write (although his formal schooling ended when he left home). He had also seen a certain character trait in his mother which may have provided him with a

THE BEGINNING: FROM DICKENS WAIF TO THE FOLLIES

comic strain he was to retain for the rest of his life. She would stand in the front doorway, greeting acquaintances, but directing low-voiced invectives in the form of asides toward her young son. Perhaps Fields' inspired but insincere heartiness, combined with his raffish two-facedness (and the low mutter and faint nervous cough of his voice), was born in that front doorway.

Fields' period of homelessness (ages eleven through fifteen) consisted of much misery and suffering. It is said that the "overdevelopment" of his nose resulted from the many street fights in which he engaged, and he was constantly exposed to the elements, which probably accounted for his husky, raspy voice. During this period, he never slept in a bed and was always sick, cold and hungry. He therefore developed a fantastic ability to cheat, steal and chisel. This may have also produced his quickness of hand which later developed into a dazzling juggling ability. In any event, saloonkeepers soon got wise to young Fields's tricks (he would buy a five-cent drink and then eat twenty-five cents' worth of free food) and chased him out of their establishments.

During this time, Fields saw the Burns Brothers, a juggling act, and his imagination was stirred. Going on the premise that he could juggle anything he could lift (including cigar boxes and every type of vegetable), he began practicing a great deal. But what may have really turned Fields onto juggling were the hours—he knew he wouldn't have to get up early in the morning and go to work. (During this period he had a job on an ice wagon and had to wake up at four A.M.)

Fields began practicing juggling intensively, sometimes as much as sixteen hours a day, and at the ripe old age of fourteen he decided that he was ready to give his first benefit performance. This event took place at Batley's Hall in Germantown, and the young performer earned almost $100—more money than he had ever seen before. Thus financially able to remove himself from his cramped and cold quarters above a wheelwright shop (where he was an honorary member of and unpaid janitor for a group known as the Orlando Social Club), young Fields moved to the unaccustomed luxury of a private room, with bed, which he rented for a dollar a week. Later in life, the pleasure of sleeping in a comfortable bed would provoke him to remark: "To this day, when I climb in bed between the sheets, I smile."

Fields read articles on juggling written by a man named Hazlitt, who treated the subject rather eloquently. He came to learn that the art of juggling consisted of the coordination of eyes, nerves and muscles in great precision. A few years later, around the turn of the century, Fields would write down his thoughts on juggling in an article called "New Juggling Tricks" in *The Magician's Handbook*. He explained his hat and cigar tricks ("the effect never fails to be justly appreciated by audiences"), and expanded further on his cigar-box juggling trick, noting that "it secures a laugh so hearty as to nearly shake the foundations of the theater when the audience sees how they have been sold."

In the middle twenties, Fields spoke of his juggling routine to a reporter, Mary B. Mullett: "You see, although my specialty was juggling, I used it only as a means to an end. I didn't just stand up and toss balls, knives, plates, and clubs. I invented little acts, which would seem like episodes out of real life, and I used my juggling to furnish the comedy element."

Fields' first paid job as a juggler was at Flynn and Grant's Park in nearby Norristown, Pennsylvania, a suburb of Philadelphia. He received five dollars a week, but the management took out $1.50 in "commissions" and Fields' carfare back and forth to his room was $3.60. Thus, he ended up each week *minus* ten cents! Nevertheless, this experience led to work on Fortesque's Pier in Atlantic City, where he juggled sometimes as much as twenty times a day and was often enlisted to do a fake "drowning" act to attract an excited crowd. (The management sold beer and sandwiches to the gawkers.) In this way, Fields picked up a few tips about hucksterism and also managed to get himself out of Philadelphia, a city for which he never had a great fondness.

But Atlantic City was just a stepping-stone to New York, where he began at a salary of eighteen dollars a week with a small road company presenting vaudeville acts and dramatic sketches. This was his first real chance to gain experience beyond juggling, since he was often enlisted to play several parts in skits. However, the tour manager absconded with the players' salaries, so they never saw any profits. Likewise a second tour with the *same* manager, and a third! This hoax stretched out to three payless seasons; but since Fields ate regularly, slept in a bed and was getting valuable experience, he really didn't mind. But he never forgot how he was cheated out of his salary, and drew upon the fraud perpetrated upon himself in later life

As a juggler in vaudeville

Young W.C. Fields

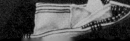

when dealing with employers, for whom he never had a high regard. In fact, he refused to trust any employer an inch, and by a combination of lying and self-promotion always managed to get more money than they had originally intended to pay. He even tried to reduce the standard ten percent agent's fee!

Fields had no love for agents, although he had a fourteen-year association with his agent and friend Bill Grady, who once remarked: "Never once in all that time did Bill ever miss a chance to cheat me if he could. When he couldn't confuse the issue to do me out of ten percent, he would reluctantly pay it, then win it back again at golf or handball—at a dollar a point."

At the same time as he was developing this suspicious attitude toward employers and agents, Fields was gaining a lot of common-sense knowledge about the inner workings of show business. He kept his eyes and ears open looking for breaks, while listening to advice from friends. (Some years later, in 1934, his friend, director Gregory La Cava, whom Fields endearingly referred to as "that Dago bastard," advised him: "Bill, you're not a natural comedian, you're a counter-puncher —the greatest straight man that ever lived. It's a mistake for you ever to do the leading. When you start to crawl out and ham around

and trip over things, you're pushing. I hate to see it.")

Whether Fields took all this advice, while developing one of the finest acts in vaudeville, is questionable. Some say he was rarely known to listen to anyone about anything, and during his rapid rise to great popularity in the thirties, it is said that he simply quit making suggestions to studio heads regarding the characters he played—he just translated his ideas into action right in front of the cameras. He discussed these matters with no one but himself!

Although Fields was presumably as wary about sex as he was about everything else, around the turn of the century he married Miss Harriet Hughes of New York City. They met while she was dancing in a musical, and although she joined his act, working with him for a few years, they were soon to separate. One son, W.C. Fields, Jr., known as Claude, was born, and Fields would send his estranged wife support money each week (as much as sixty dollars but never more) for the rest of his life. Their wrangling—usually over money, while separated by a great many miles—continued until the end of his life. During his *Follies* career, Fields met and lived on Long Island with a Ziegfeld girl named Bessie Poole. It is widely rumored that she had a son by him during the seven years they lived

Rehearsing for the 1925 edition of the Ziegfeld Follies with Ray Dooley. Chorine Cricket Wooten looks on.

together.

In 1898, Fields wrote his mother a letter, enclosing ten dollars. This was the first the family had heard of him in nearly ten years. From then on, Fields would send his mother at least ten dollars each week until she died. And contrary to what has generally been written, Fields became devoted to his mother and later in life even treated his father to a world tour. When he visited them in Philadelphia, it was always with a flourish, arriving in a rented Packard touring car—most likely for the benefit of nosey neighbors.

After five years, Fields began getting some of the best vaudeville bookings and spent a large part of his early professional life abroad (Europe, South Africa, the South Sea Islands, among other places) as a juggler and pantomimist, soon becoming known as "America's

Greatest Comedy Juggler."

In London, during one of his performances, King Edward VII sat in one of the boxes with a group of friends. The King liked Fields so much that he invited him to perform at Buckingham Palace for a gala function—an honor afforded only one other performer on the program, Sarah Bernhardt. Later, when asked about this auspicious moment, Fields would say: "In my opinion, that Edward was a majestic man." He delighted in repeating the story of this performance to friends, although he did not hesitate to express his annoyance at the English people for what he felt was their overly abiding trust in the basic decency of human nature, a characteristic he considered singularly feeble-minded on their part.

Perhaps the most important aspect of these early vaudeville years was that Fields became a master of pantomime, an art which could be appreciated in any part of the world without the intrusion of a language barrier. This would be of enormous help as his entrance into the world of silent films drew near.

In 1914, Fields spent a record twenty-nine days traveling from Australia back to New York, having received an offer from C.B. Dillingham to appear in *Watch Your Step*, a revue starring Vernon and Irene Castle, with music by Irving Berlin. But Fields was dropped after only one day's out-of-town performance. Nevertheless, the strenuous return trip to America was not in vain. Gene Buck, a Ziegfeld scout, spotted Fields and signed him with the *Follies*, where he was to develop and refine his act as a "prop comedian." It was during his early *Follies* days that Bill Fields met his longtime agent, Bill Grady.

As a pantomimist, Fields delighted in getting his audience to the point where the entire house would be breathlessly watching him—winning them gradually, and finally achieving all of their concentrated attention. Although largely a comedy pantomimist, Fields incorporated a great deal of improvisation into his routine, such as dropping both his cigar and hat during his juggling routine and then flawlessly maneuvering them back onto their proper places. He interspersed his gambling act with acrobatics and pantomime novelties, and soon created a burlesque golf game which later would be incorporated into several of his feature films.

Fields' co-stars in the *Follies* were many of the leading comedians of the day, including Fanny Brice, Bert Williams, Eddie Cantor (who once told friends that Fields read Shakespeare, Chaucer and Milton plus most of Dickens' novels while they were on tour), Will Rogers, and Ed Wynn. On one

With Ziegfeld girls at a rehearsal of the 1925 Follies

occasion in Boston, while performing the billiard act (which Fields
had thoroughly perfected), Wynn
hid under the pool table. Unknown
to Fields, Wynn began stealing
laughs from Fields who soon
realized that something was awry
since the added laughs were not expected. He smacked Wynn on the
head with a cue stick, to the

audience's delight. Later, Fields
tried to persuade Wynn to incorpo-
rate the unexpected routine per-
manently into the act, but Wynn
refused politely.

Fields' first film, *Pool Sharks*, was
made for the Gaumont Company in
1915. He had worked up his greatest routine, the trick pool table,
during his vaudeville years in

American and European music halls and theaters. Ever since he had racked balls as a boy, the game of pool fascinated Fields. For his act, he had a special table constructed, to which he kept adding gimmicks. The most effective gimmick of all, of course, was the last "defeated" desperate shot, which sent all fifteen balls scurrying around—all of them winding up in the pockets (courtesy of invisible threads and extraordinary handling), to the amazement of audiences. It was an exquisite pantomime performance by a genuine artist. That same year he made another silent short, *His Lordship's Dilemma;* unfortunately, no prints of this film are known to have survived.

What we can see in Fields' first experience with the new medium of motion pictures is his remarkable sense of timing and his skilled powers of understatement. Although these were developed on the stage, they came across with remarkable naturalness on screen. In *Pool Sharks,* within the framework of his antic horseplay and the sense of timing he must have developed and perfected as a juggler (where seconds are sliced to mini-seconds), the art of W.C. Fields is quite clear.

Fields went back to the *Follies,* however, and did not make another picture for ten years. One day, he noticed William Blanche, a stagehand of somewhat bizarre appearance—he was a dwarf with an enormous head. Blanche became Fields' caddy in his famous golf act, and the two worked well together.

A master showman whose *Follies* extravaganzas were popular theater attractions for many years, Florenz Ziegfeld was not known for his fondness toward comedians. Ziegfeld once infuriated Fields by sitting quietly through an elaborate comedy routine. Afterwards, he asked an assistant: "How long does it take the girls to dress here?" Told it took seven minutes, Ziegfeld ordered Fields to hold his sketch to exactly that length. Needless to say, Fields was angry.

But throughout this period with the *Follies* (he was in every edition from 1915 through 1921), Fields made the best of what he must have sometimes considered a trying business. And he was beginning to earn substantial amounts of money: during his *Follies* years, his weekly salary rose from two hundred dollars to several thousand. He is widely known to have acted in an eccentric way about his money (his mother brought him up to distrust banks), often carrying large sums on his person. (When he left New York City for California in 1931, he drove with his pockets lined with thousand-dollar bills to the grand tune of $350,000.) When traveling, he opened bank accounts all over

POOL SHARKS (1915). Fields does his pool routine.

the country and the world under fictitious names (his penchant for outrageous pseudonyms was to extend later to his authoring of screenplays), and although we can assume he knew what amounts of money he had and where they were located, it is said that before his death Fields destroyed all records of these savings accounts. His family estimated that he may have had as much as $1,000,000 in hidden bank accounts, probably lost to them forever! Fields, no doubt, would have been pleased by his family's frustration at this loss—and perhaps planned it that way.

After his long stint with the *Follies*, Fields spent a year in George White's *Scandals* before winning the role of Eustace McGargle, a fraud dear to Fields' heart, in the Broadway musical, *Poppy*. He was an ideal choice for the character—a petty show-business con man—and succeeded

24

in creating one of the classic roles of the American theater. With his audacious top hat, baggy pants, and fraudulent moustache, he rejuvenated ancient slapstick into something fresh and original. Audiences were mesmerized by this artful schemer who tried to pass off his adopted daughter (Madge Kennedy) as an heiress.*

The role was a turning point in Fields' career, and, curiously, he was never again to drift too far from its basic outline. *Poppy* opened at the New Apollo Theater in New York on September 3, 1923 and was a great success. But Fields was more than a success—he was a sensation for both audiences and critics. The *New York Tribune* reviewer concluded his comments on Fields' performance by saying: "We suspect him to be the funniest man in town since Will Rogers went away." The show ran for over a year, and led to his starring in D.W. Griffith's film version of the stage play, retitled *Sally of the Sawdust.*

*Lyricist Howard Deitz wrote Fields' dialogue and one song, all without program credit.

On the set of POPPY (1936).

In 1925 Fields had a small part as a British sergeant in William Randolph Hearst's film production, *Janice Meredith*, an historical epic set during the American Revolutionary War. The picture starred Hearst's protégée Marion Davies and, regrettably, has not been preserved in its entirety today. Later that year, Fields made *Sally of the Sawdust* which, happily, is wonderfully preserved.

Produced by Griffith at Paramount's Long Island studios, this film was generally well received by audiences and critics, although some writers complained about the film's continuity and editing, calling it "sloppy" and not up to the director's usual high standards.

Nevertheless, its popular appeal was more than justified by the introduction of Fields in his first starring role. His personality came across loud and clear (even without sound), and although many felt that Griffith reworked the story somewhat to allow co-star Carol Dempster, a Griffith favorite, to get a major share of screen time, whenever Fields is on-screen, he dominates the proceedings. There are several quick shots of his juggling routines (Griffith, unfortunately, cuts away too quickly, too often) and only once in the film—during the initial carnival sequence—does Griffith allow Fields the luxury of sustained close-ups of his deft juggling. Yet

THE SILENT FILMS: JUGGLING PAYS OFF

Fields emerges with a good deal of his forceful presence intact.

Those who worked on the film reported that Griffith and Fields frequently disagreed during the shooting. This is not surprising, since Fields' freewheeling independence and high-jinks style could hardly mesh with Griffith's highly disciplined work methods. Yet the two did collaborate the following year on *That Royle Girl*, again costarring Carol Dempster, so they must have compromised their differences for the sake of professional survival. (Unfortunately, no prints of *That Royle Girl* are extant.)

The best scene in *Sally of the Sawdust* is the one in which McGargle is accidentally locked inside an oven. Just before he is almost burned to a crisp, his daughter Sally saves him, pulling him out to safety. While readjusting his apparel (his trousers are still smoldering), Fields becomes aware that his daughter is growing up. (Or at least he *thinks* she is. Sally, always thinking about the future, has stuffed several baker's buns into her bosom.) Fields' underplaying works well with the attractive Miss Dempster's endearing style, and the scene is both charming and funny.

JANICE MEREDITH (1925). With Marion Davies

Interestingly, a good part of the movie was shot outdoors (Harry Fischbeck's camerawork is excellent), so that we really get a feeling and flavor for the mid-twenties Long Island countryside. (Ironically, the later version of *Poppy*, shot in Hollywood in 1936, seems fake, largely because it was made on a studio set.)

Despite the fact that we are not allowed the pleasure of the Fieldsian dialogue, his presence—the favorite sight gags which were to become so familiar and loved later on—and his engaging screen personality make the film an impressive first success. There's even a moment when Fields gets a chance to kick a dog—thus beginning a long tradition of dog abuse on screen. And there are hilarious lines, flashed on title cards, such as the one where Fields, seeing the "villain," Judge Foster, says: "He's got a face that looks like it wore out four bodies!"

Another marvelous scene occurs when Fields, playing a game of three-card monte, is approached by the local constable and quickly devises an escape by wrapping himself in an Indian blanket. At the film's climax, there is an elaborate car chase which causes Fields to be late for his appearance before the judge who has detained Sally. Arriving on the scene, Fields tells the judge:

"I'd have been here sooner, but I was thrown by a Ford."

In the end, the film seems to take on an almost Chaplinesque air—but not quite. As Fields walks off alone with his derby and cane, Sally runs to stop him, brings him back, and in the final scene we see that he has apparently become a successful businessman by going into the real estate business. This is in line with a consistent Fieldsian theme, that of raising the ante in his "game" of making a sucker of anyone he can con. As earlier in the film, when he was accused of cheating in gambling, the final title tells it all: "It's the old Army game," says Fields with a delicious wink.

For the next three years, from 1926 to 1928, Fields starred in eight feature films, many shot at the Long Island studios where William LeBaron was production head. The films, all about one hour long, are: *It's the Old Army Game, That Royle Girl, So's Your Old Man, Running Wild, Two Flaming Youths, The Potters, Tillie's Punctured Romance* and *Fools For Luck.* Until recently, it was thought that most of them did not survive; however, in the last few years, prints have been discovered of all but *That Royle Girl.*

Many of these silent movies were later remade by Fields as sound films. *So's Your Old Man* was remade in 1934 as *You're Telling Me;*

SALLY OF THE SAWDUST (1925). As Professor McGargle

Running Wild became *Man on the Flying Trapeze* in 1935; elements of *It's the Old Army Game* were later seen in *It's a Gift* (1934); and the best parts of *Two Flaming Youths* were later to appear in two Fields remakes, *The Old-Fashioned Way* (1934) and *You Can't Cheat an Honest Man* (1939). *Tillie's Punctured Romance* was itself a silent remake of the earlier popular Sennett silent film.

Probably the most successful of the lot, and the one in which Fields gave his best performance is *The Potters* (1927), about an average family and the difficulties that arise when "Pa" Potter (Fields) gullibly invests four thousand dollars of the family savings in some worthless oil stock without "Ma's" (Mary Alden) consent. (Things end on a happy note, however, when new oil is found in the old wells and the family becomes rich.) Most reviewers were enthusiastic about the film and singled out Fields for praise. *The New York Times'* movie critic Mordaunt Hall wrote:

> Mr. Fields' portrayal of "Pa" Potter is a joy, a characterization which reveals that this stage veteran has studied his previous film work and checked his extravagant tendencies.

SALLY OF THE SAWDUST (1925). With Carol Dempster

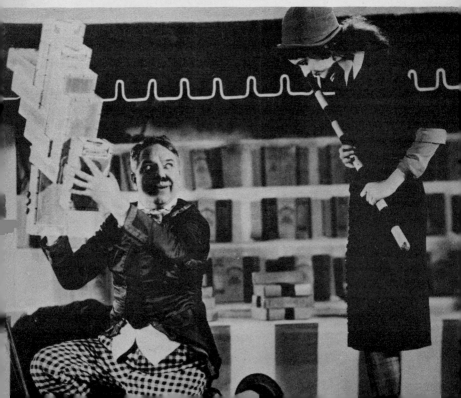

SALLY OF THE SAWDUST (1925). With Carol Dempster

So well suited to this part is Mr. Fields that one wonders whether anyone could ever have rivaled his performance.*

LeBaron and Fields got along quite well, since the executive believed in giving his players a good deal of freedom—much more than they would have had at the West Coast studios. He put Fields under contract, and between 1925 and 1938, LeBaron produced more than twenty Fields films.

It's the Old Army Game, released in 1926, co-starred Louise Brooks and was Fields' first collaboration with director Edward Sutherland, once a Sennett leading man. The two became good friends, and went on to work together on *Tillie's Punctured Romance* (1928), *Mississippi* (1935), *Poppy* (1936), and *Follow the Boys* (1944). Miss Brooks, in a reminiscence about Fields and their work on the film, wrote: "Fields is perhaps the only comedian who reveals, through his stately procedures, the passionate amount of work he puts into his performances."**

As the somewhat pretentious title card suggested at the beginning of *It's the Old Army Game*, it was an "epic of the American druggist —whose shop is the social center,

*January 18, 1927

**Louise Brooks, "The Other Face of W.C. Fields," *Sight and Sound*, Spring, 1971.

31

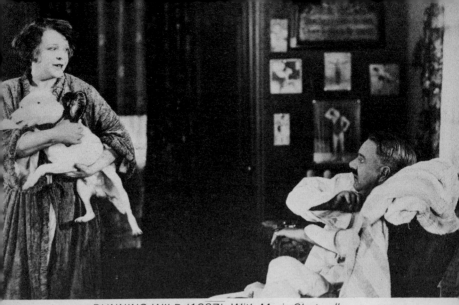

RUNNING WILD (1927). With Marie Shotwell

place of countless conveniences and a forum of public thought—the druggist who is the agent between life and death." W.C. Fields, as the druggist Elmer Prettywillie, complete with clip-on moustache and top hat, was basically a humanitarian, with an eye toward that elusive "good life," although at the film's end he makes this moral comment: "A bird in the hand is a hard pill to swallow. In a word, never give a sucker an even break—it's the old Army game."

Fields would repeat his druggist role later in *The Pharmacist*, a two-reeler for Sennett, and in the sound feature, *It's a Gift*, many of the silent film's story elements would be duplicated. Miss Brooks does nicely as the young girl who works at Mr. Prettywillie's counter. One hilarious scene involves Fields pulling a fake fire alarm in order to get rid of several firemen who are customers in his store, in order to focus all his attentions on the girl at the counter. But when a *real* fire starts, Fields makes a riotous attempt to put it out with nothing more than glasses of water.

The movie also features a forerunner of the famous porch-sleeping sequence in *It's a Gift*, complete with a ruckus brought on by an ornery baby (*not* Baby LeRoy, this time) who breaks a bottle over Fields' head. Undaunted by the child, who thinks Fields is his uncle, Prettywillie retorts: "Uncle will give you some nice razor blades to play with!" Other disturbing

THE POTTERS (1927). With Mary Alden

TILLIE'S PUNCTURED ROMANCE (1928). With Babe London

events on the porch include a noisy vegetable man, a persistent scissors-grinder, and a bothersome iceman. Finally, Fields pulls out his rifle, but it unexpectedly backfires as his hammock collapses.

Later, back at the drugstore, Fields is hounded by an odd assortment of customers who demand two cents' worth of stamps (from the *middle* of the sheet, no less!), insist on splitting a box of Smith Bros. cough drops to be *delivered*, and by a sheriff who has his eye on an exotic elixir. As with most Fields films, small-town Americana is seen at its worst and funniest, and its middle-class mores are sardonically debunked as Fields has a field day conniving most of the local yokels. As one title card sums it up: "There's one born every minute —so the daylight savings law provided Prettywillie with sixty more suckers a day!"

The film's highlights include a shell game masterminded by Fields, and a lovely April Fool's Day holiday outing (it is said that off-screen Fields delighted in such picnic outings) during which the Prettywillie family, consisting of wife, sister, nephew and other assorted relatives, camps out on private grounds. They manage to turn a beautiful lawn into a trash heap, as Fields comments: "A motorist has no rights anymore—imagine a man building a house in the middle of a beautiful lawn like this!" As the butler chases them away, Fields remarks: "He's just a servant." (Off-screen Fields never got along with servants, and his friends would often remark how he delighted in turning them against each other.)

The plot takes a turn for the bizarre as Fields, having been duped into selling bogus lots to local customers, goes to New York City to make things right with the "High and Dry Realty Company." In the end, things *do* manage to work out all right (the lots are worth money, after all), as Field remarks, with a wink in his eye, to the local sheriff, "I never told a lie in my life." Appropriately, a portrait of George Washington falls off the wall behind him!

Later that same year, Fields made *So's Your Old Man*. Directed by Gregory La Cava, the film featured Fields as one Samuel Brisbee, an inventor living in the town of Waukeagus, who created the non-breakable windshield for automobiles. (The same theme was to be repeated in *Man on the Flying Trapeze*, with puncture-proof tires substituted for the windshield.) The movie makes several pointed comments about class distinctions—the Brisbees are *not* from the "right" side of the railroad tracks, so to speak—and Fields delights in debunking upper-class mores.

Early in the film, he enters the

IT'S THE OLD ARMY GAME (1926). With Louise Brooks

IT'S THE OLD ARMY GAME (1926). With Blanche Ring, Mary Foy, and Mickey Bennett

house, just as his wife, a humble sort (played by Marcia Harris) is trying to practice the social graces with a high-society matron whose son is romancing the Brisbee daughter. Fields, dirty and wearing an undershirt, spots the upper-class biddy and says: "I knew your old man when he had only one pair of pants." Calling Brisbee "a vulgarian," she huffs as he quickly retorts: "So's your old man!" while his wife pro-

ceeds to chase him out of the house.

Fields next goes to Washington, where he tells a convention of automobile engineers, "This glass of mine is harder to break than a blonde's heart." Unfortunately, through a mix-up involving a switch of cars, he demonstrates its "non-breakability" on the wrong automobile, and goes back home empty-handed and dejected. On the train, he strikes up a friendship with a genuine princess named Lescaboura (Alice Joyce). Town gossips who see the two talking assume the worst and spread the word around town that Sam has committed a moving violation of his marriage vows.

Later, the princess helps Fields by coming to Waukeagus and asking for him personally. Society matrons are duly impressed, and Fields even manages to dedicate the new golf links, teeing off the first ball with delight, as the princess and bewildered neighbors look on. This premise, of course, provides Fields with an excuse to do his entire golf routine, as the princess watches. Fields, apparently still not realizing that she really *is* royalty, remarks slyly: "This princess idea is great stuff, if they don't get wise to us."

In the end, all turns out for the best as the engineers realize their mistake and offer Brisbee a one-

SO'S YOUR OLD MAN (1926). With Julia Ralph and Marcia Harris

SO'S YOUR OLD MAN (1926). With Frank Montgomery and Alice Joyce

million-dollar contract—after first chasing him all over the golf links into a pond.

The last scene shows Fields and family now "socially acceptable" and rich. Fields, removing a good portion of his stuffy tuxedo in front of a bevy of butlers, tells them: "If anybody wants me, I'll be in the garage for the next two weeks," and he strolls off with two old cronies —the three of them side-by-side with bottles in hand.

During this period, Fields revised stories and improvised his characters in order to include whole sections of his Ziegfeld act and some vaudeville routines. It is said that he told La Cava that he would have to include his golf act in *So's Your Old Man*. When the director reminded the star that the movie was about a princess, and that there was neither room nor reason in the film for a golf act, Fields shot back: "The princess can play the caddie," and the act got

FOOLS FOR LUCK (1928). With Mary Alden and Jack Luden

into the film.

Fields made five more films for the studio in the next two years (*Running Wild, Two Flaming Youths, The Potters, Tillie's Punctured Romance* and *Fools for Luck*), but when his contract ran out in 1928 it was not renewed—most likely because of the star's somewhat bizarre approach to moviemaking. The films did not make much money, although they were considered artistic successes. Fields, however, *did* make money, and was undaunted by this period of movie unemployment. He enjoyed his leisure time by playing golf and pressing his agent, Bill Grady, to find work for him.

Finally, an offer came from Earl Carroll, an ex-Ziegfeld performer, for Fields to star in the 1928 edition of his *Vanities* for the startling sum of $6,500 a week, plus substantial bonuses and percentages. Fields was a great success back on Broadway, doing variations of his old routines, ad-libbing in skits with other players, and generally being his usual unflappable self. He even took special delight in arranging for Carroll's name to be removed from the marquee and replacing it with his own.

As the twenties came to a close, Fields was well into middle age, in fact, approaching fifty. Although he hadn't set the movie world on fire, he somehow knew that his future was to lie in the world of films —especially now that sound had arrived.

Fields left the East Coast—lock, stock and barrel—in 1931, driving across the country in his new Lincoln with $350,000 in thousand-dollar bills stashed throughout his person—not bad for a runaway kid who didn't have a bed to sleep in for several years and whose formal education had stopped at age eleven. Fields often tried to give friends the impression he had lost "everything" in the stock-market crash of 1929, but they knew better than to believe that he would have trusted the market (or anything) enough to invest his entire nest egg in it.

Actually, Fields was risking much more than money: he was leaving the stage and New York forever, closing one long chapter in his life and turning the pages to an unknown medium and a new life—one in which his security might be, at best, dubious. He was, in a sense, starting from professional scratch and for the courage of such a drastic move, W. C. Fields deserves a great deal of admiration.

His "arrival" in Hollywood is now legendary: he entered a lavish Hollywood hotel and asked for the bridal suite; not surprisingly, the management refused to give it to him. Undaunted, he was soon ensconced in a rented mansion on Toluca Lake with no firm movie offers in hand. His somewhat unorthodox reputation had apparently preceded him,

FROM NEW YORK TO CALIFORNIA: THE FIRST TALKIES

and he remained out of work for some months. This didn't seem to bother him, and he spent much of his time on the golf links and with friends Greg La Cava and Eddie Sutherland (who was directing for Paramount), LeBaron (who was working for RKO), his old agent Bill Grady (now with MGM), writer Gene Fowler, and Mack Sennett. He also became quite fond of eating at Dave Chasen's restaurant in Hollywood.

Before joining forces with Mack Sennett to make four two-reelers, Fields made his first sound film, a short for RKO called *The Golf Specialist* (1930), followed by his first full-length sound feature for Warner Bros., *Her Majesty, Love* (1931).

The Golf Specialist was the ideal showcase for Fields' talents. Essentially an extended vaudeville act, the short film is curiously uncinematic (it is photographed mostly as a straight stage routine), but nevertheless provides us with a good record of the famous golf routine intact. This is the same routine which Fields put together in vaudeville and brought to the *Follies*. It consisted of a golf bag three times the ordinary size; a

THE GOLF SPECIALIST (1930).

HER MAJESTY, LOVE (1931). With Marilyn Miller and Leon Errol

driver with a rubber shaft (which would wrap itself around his neck when he took a heavy swing); a garden hoe and shovel for sand traps; a buggy whip for unattentive caddies; an unattentive caddy; plus other assorted items such as a polo mallet, trick rubber trees, a wind velocity indicator, a tripod and, of course, a cocktail shaker.

The opening scene reveals Fields as J. Effington Bellwether (looking very dapper with moustache, cane and straw hat), being evasive to the hotel clerk who appears concerned about several overdue rent bills.

Fields spots a little girl with a piggy bank and makes a vain attempt to steal it. As the girl screams, he says, "She probably has a pin stuck in her." He also flirts with the house detective's attractive blonde wife. At one point, she remarks to him: "You have courage written all over you." Fields retorts: "It's the laundry marks, my dear."

On the links, Fields is almost upstaged by his caddy—a man with annoyingly squeaky shoes and a strange voice, and no concern for Fields' hat (which he steps on, at one point). Obviously miffed at the man, Fields huffs: "I wouldn't have him again as my caddy for all the tea—er, chop suey in China." And there's even a bit of sexual innuendo when Fields' blonde companion watches his golf swing and notes wryly: "He *is* quite a driver."

In the end, the local sheriff finally catches up with J. Effington Bellwether, and it's worth repeating the catalogue of offenses for which Fields is being pursued:

Bigamy
Passing as the Prince of Wales
Eating spaghetti in public
Using hard words in a speakeasy
Trumping a partner's ace
Spitting in the Gulf Stream
Jumping the board bill in seventeen lunatic asylums
Failure to pay installments on a strait-jacket
Possession of a skunk
Revealing the facts of life to an Indian

As the sheriff handcuffs Fields and leads him away, we hear Fields muttering to himself, "keep the wrists close together . . ." while ignoring the sheriff. Obviously, his

HER MAJESTY, LOVE (1931). Rehearsing on the set

mind is still on the golf game.

Her Majesty, Love is one of Fields' oddest and, curiously, most touching works. It is generally not considered one of his best roles (he is billed as a supporting player to Marilyn Miller), and it is not often quoted by most Fields buffs. Nevertheless, its charm is undeniable, and it marked Fields as a major talent in sound films.

German director William Dieterle helmed the picture, giving it a strong Germanic flavor. In fact, the locale (although strictly Hollywood backlot) is supposed to be Berlin during the decadent thirties. But most audiences could never forget for a minute that these were American actors playing in an American film. Fields doesn't appear on-screen until twenty-five minutes of the film have elapsed. At first, he vainly attempts to render a German accent; but, as the movie progresses, he gradually loosens up, and finally drops the affectation.

Still wearing a moustache (which he kept all during his silent-film period), Fields plays the part of the coarse but sly father—a barber by profession—of a girl (Miss Miller) who tends bar in a cabaret. Having spent most of his life as a juggler with a traveling show (the part was obviously tailored to suit Fields' special abilities), he can't resist doing a little juggling with some chocolate eclairs—and anything

else that comes into his range.

As in so many of Fields' films, there is the theme of lower-versus-upper class conflict. In this case, his daughter meets a wealthy and handsome young man whose family disapproves of the two marrying. With the engagement off, Miss Miller (with some prodding by her father) decides to accept the importunings of a wealthy baron and marries him. But on their wedding night, her true love comes back to her, and they go off together—leaving behind the baron, the startled wedding guests, and Fields.

One of the best scenes in the film takes place at an elaborate banquet given by the family of his daughter's fiancé. At an enormous table, Fields does a marvelous balancing act, juggling food onto his plate, eating with his gloves on (the upper-crust folk are aghast!) and drinking heavily. As he tells the astonished guests that his little barber shop "doesn't bring in much these days—everyone's got a safety razor," Fields begins to throw food to the family members, telling them that he learned his "tricks" in the circus. He ends up by juggling plates and oranges and—as he leaves—he tips the butler with a sneer.

Realizing that his daughter's engagement to the rich young man is doomed, Fields encourages his daughter to accept the baron's offer of marriage with the comment: "He's a great catch—he's rich and old—and you can always look forward to a happy widowhood." Later, hoping for a little of the baron's loot for himself, Fields tells him: "I had the devil's own time getting my daughter to marry you . . ."

Although the film is a seriously intended romance, with lovely musical interludes, Fields' characterization of the father gives it a whole new tone and exuberance. Dieterle's direction is expert and the camerawork is exciting (mobile, never static). The early scenes of Miss Miller and Fields together in their ramshackle apartment are both touching and joyful. Whenever Fields appears, his amusing byplay lifts the film into a realm far above its standard genre of the romantic musical. Many of the typical Fieldsian themes (the special tenderness between father and daughter) and scenes such as the disastrous banquet would appear again in later Fields films. (The banquet turned up as an engagement party in *You Can't Cheat an Honest Man*.)

But in this, his first feature sound film, Fields is the true heart and life of the movie. And although he seems to disappear somewhat from the climactic romantic scenes, this film would re-establish his reputation as a screen actor. It was his best, most critically acclaimed role since *The Potters*, and led to an important new movie career.

Although it is generally believed that Fields' deal with Mack Sennett put him back on his feet, the facts are otherwise. Fields had already completed two features for Paramount in 1932 (*Million Dollar Legs* and a cameo role in *If I Had a Million*) before making the first of four two-reelers for Sennett. What the Sennett films probably did achieve was to save Fields from being treated like many of the other Paramount stars of the time. They were not usually given as free a hand in choosing their material as was Fields.

His contract with Sennett guaranteed him $5000 per week, plus certain fringe benefits. The two managed to get along well, despite their contrasting views: Fields believed that movie comedy did not require a finely honed hairline construction; Sennett felt that comedy should be created much like an intricate mechanism.

During the course of filming one of these comedy shorts, Fields was the victim of an accident on the set—a truck driven by a prop man backed into him and broke his neck, causing a hospital stay highlighted by his friends' daily trips back and forth with smuggled liquor. During the early part of his hospital stay, Fields—always irrepressible—

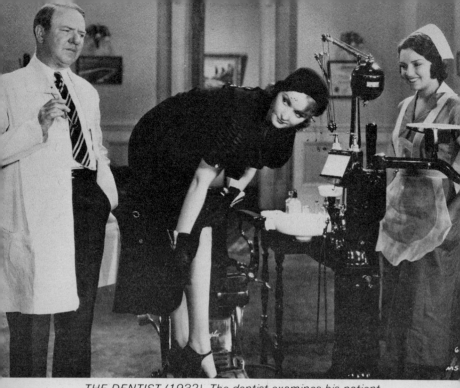

THE DENTIST (1932). The dentist examines his patient.

somehow drove his wheelchair down a flight of stairs, compounding his injuries (he fractured his coccyx) and extending his stay to two months. Of this, he complained: "I went in broken at one end, and they treated me by breaking the other." Perhaps Fields' cynicism, which extended from studio heads down to property men, was justified. In any case, he delighted in recalling similar stories of near-tragedies (most of them fabricated) such as the time that a prop man accidentally threw him to three lions during the filming of *Tillie's Punctured Romance*. For-

tunately, Fields emerged unscathed, although he (and later his various biographers) enjoyed creating ghastly-sounding stories about this and other near-fatal experiences on movie sets.

The first of the four Sennett comedies (all of which were written by him) was *The Dentist* (1932). As with the other shorts, the film's length (twenty minutes) and construction meshed perfectly with the Fieldsian style—their brevity and lack of subplots offered Fields an opportunity to develop each nuance and to pace every insulting comment with precision, allowing the right amount of time for each expression and gesture to register. As with the best of his feature films, the basic theme concerned a man's small wars against a hostile world and his frustration in the face of seemingly diabolical forces. Throughout these two-reelers, Fields draws a deadly bead on a number of middle-class stupidities and pieties.

The Dentist is, of course, Fields. He's somewhat absent-minded and makes his own rules—like playing a round of golf before his first appointment. Back at his waiting room, we see a woman screaming in pain. Fields' reaction to her is entirely nonchalant as he remarks, "I don't believe in doctors—a doctor right down the street treated a man for yellow jaundice, then found out he was a Jap!" (Fields' distrust of doctors in real life was legendary.) There's a good bit of raunchy sexual innuendo as a woman enters complaining that a dog has bitten her on the leg. Fields, ignoring the leg, inspects her more curvaceous areas. At one point he asks her whether she would like him to use gas or not. She answers: "Gas or electric light—I'd feel nervous having you fool around with me in the dark."

Fields also treats his nurse with some disdain and has little use for his patients, referring to them as "buzzards and palookas" and to his

dental instrument as a "buzz saw." At another point, Fields becomes entangled with another attractive patient who wraps her long legs around him while he pulls her tooth. (Some of this footage was probably left on the cutting-room floor, since it was quite risqué.)

The Dentist's subplot deals with Fields' daughter and her romance with an iceman, and there's also a very funny scene with a bearded man who enters Fields' office, only to be greeted by the question: "How's everything in Moscow?" Fields has trouble finding the man's mouth, finally applying a stethoscope in his search.

The picture is hilarious throughout its short running time (Fields also gets in a bit of practicing with his duck-hunting gun) and is a worthy showcase for the comedian's outrageous wit. The bite of its humor is unusual, however, in that—unlike the other three Sennett shorts —in *The Dentist* Fields portrays the central character in a wholly unappealing light—he is inconsiderate, cruel and somewhat of a cheat. This aspect would be played down in the remaining three two-reelers which were warmer in overall tone, but no less uproarious as a display of Fields' personal style.

A few months later, *The Fatal Glass of Beer* was released, burlesquing Victorian sentimentality and morality. In its initial showing,

49

THE FATAL GLASS OF BEER (1933). With George Chandler

the film was not received well by audiences—although it is probably the most brilliant of the four and has since become the best known. The madcap plot, or nonplot, caught Fields in top form and he energetically thrust himself into the film's eccentric black-comedy world. Fields is an Alaskan trapper who lives in a log cabin and tells wild tales about his son's being lured to ruin through drink (of all things!) in the big city.* This is retold in flashback style, but the comedy makes no attempt at realism. As Fields mushes his dog team, the back projection is ludicrous, and the snow looks like (and *is*) cornflakes. Fields sits down to a most unappetizing-looking meal with his downtrodden wife (Rosemary Theby) who tells him that another creditor is on their trail and that this time he may take the dog team.

Then their son Chester (George Chandler) returns home from prison, where he had been sent for stealing some bonds. In a turnabout climax, both Fields and his wife cast Chester off into the snowy wastes, complaining that he has only come back "to sponge off us for the rest of your life." Fields' last classic comment, "It ain't a fit night out for man nor beast!" is *not* followed by the expected handful of snow

*At one point, Fields remarks: "I think I'll go out and milk my elk."

(cornflakes) thrown in his face, as was done throughout the film.

Exhibitors complained that *The Fatal Glass of Beer* was "a waste of twenty minutes of film." One theater owner called it "the worst comedy we have played from any company this season—no story, no acting, and as a whole—nothing." Fields would probably have been delighted by this reaction, and then pronounce it to be the correct one. As a matter of fact, he makes his own assessment of the bogus backgrounds" in the film itself when, driving his dog team, he looks at the snow and slyly addresses the audience: "Looks more like cornflakes!"

The Fatal Glass of Beer was probably a sideswipe at Chaplin's *The Gold Rush* (1925). Fields had worked with Chaplin in the Folies Bergére, where he appeared as a star with top billing, while Chaplin was just beginning his career. Many years later, Fields was presuaded by a friend to see one of Chaplin's films after Charlie had become a big star. Fields walked out halfway through, and his only comment is said to have been, "He's nothing but a goddamn ballet dancer." This critique on Chaplin sounds about right for Fields, whose films generally stayed away from pathos. Rather, they concentrated on the plight of the common man suffering from the eternal paranoia of being

THE FATAL GLASS OF BEER (1933). Fields confronts the Indians.

put upon by friends, foes, fate and governments. Audiences could really identify with this poor, harassed soul.

Fields' last two Sennett comedies were *The Barber Shop* and *The Pharmacist*. Both were made in 1933 and were a cut above their predecessors in production values and visual style. *The Pharmacist* displays many of Fields' standard themes and routines, as it accurately burlesques small-town Americana. Fields, as Dr. Dilwog, has a wife and two daughters who are the bane of his existence. The elder one talks endlessly on the telephone to her boyfriend Cuthbert (Grady Sutton) while the younger daughter refuses to eat her spinach and swallows the pet canary instead.

The drugstore does a booming stamp business, and there are a couple of routines which are repeated later in *It's a Gift* (1934). The film features a wild climax, as a gun battle develops in the store between an escaping gunman and the police. Fields is "rescued" by Cuthbert, who will apparently become his son-in-law. The brightest moment in the movie occurs when Fields' younger daughter (Babe Kane) mixes his martini by bouncing up and down on a pogo stick—a singularly novel idea.

The Barber Shop featured Fields as O'Hair, a small-town barber with a beastly wife and an eye for his

THE PHARMACIST (1933). Fields with a customer

pretty manicurist. Similar to *The Pharmacist* in its hair-raising ending (Fields captures a bank robber, accidentally), the movie arouses our sympathy for this henpecked man who resorts to playing a bass fiddle (which he affectionately refers to as "Leona") for relaxation. The film's high point occurs when Fields reduces an obese man to a mere shadow in his steam room, later remarking: "I've never hurt man, beast or child—except when I've had to." He then proceeds to shave a customer, asking: "Got a mole?" The customer answers, "I've had it all my life." To which Fields responds, "You won't have it anymore."

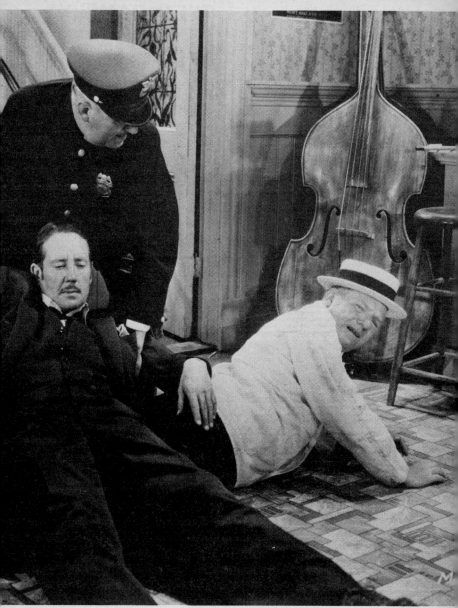

THE BARBER SHOP (1933). Fields captures a bank robber (accidentally).

The reputation of his four Mack Sennett comedy shorts revived Fields' somewhat sluggish movie career and gave him the kind of audience recognition he had not yet attained. Before ending his association with Sennett (an amicable break for both, apparently), Fields had completed two roles for Paramount. The first was a cameo performance (with Alison Skipworth) in *If I Had a Million* (1932), a multi-segmented, star-heavy feature. The second was a genuine star performance in *Million Dollar Legs* (1932), probably one of the most artful films in which Fields would appear throughout his career.

While Fields was making *Million Dollar Legs*, he noticed a singer and dancer named Carlotta Monti who had a small part in the film. Through an elaborate plot set up by a somewhat embarrassed Fields, he met this Mexican-Italian beauty who was to live with him as friend, confidante and mistress until his death in 1946.

At Paramount, Fields did not have the kind of free hand with his material that he would later exercise at Universal. But *Million Dollar Legs*, directed by Edward Cline and based on an original story by Joseph L. Mankiewicz, rivaled the studio's Ernst Lubitsch comedies in satire and charm, with a helping of genuine farce added for good meas-

THE PARAMOUNT YEARS: UPS AND DOWNS

ure. Its zaniness resembled the Marx Brothers' *Duck Soup*, and it has grown in reputation through the years. (Today, some critics even consider it a genuine comic masterpiece of "American Dadaism".)

The film, however, cannot really be considered a true Fields classic, since he exercised minimal off-screen control over it. It consists of a succession of outrageous sight gags with Fields contributing the ultimate outrage when he performs as a weight-lifter in the Los Angeles Olympics. As president of a mythical and bankrupt country—Klopstockia—Fields arm wrestles with the secretary of treasury (Hugh Herbert) and, for the first time, appears without that strange little moustache and battered straw hat (replaced by a bedraggled top hat) he was to cling to for so long. This overall change in appearance drew audiences closer to the image of Fields as a legitimate "family man"—a person who was often a victim fighting for his dignity.

The film's fanciful imagination and freshness of style includes a takeoff on crazy bureaucratic governments (Klopstockia elects its presidents by arm-pulling contests) and a touch of Mata Hari satire. (There are several mysterious spies, including one attractive female who sings.) The film's reckless abandon barely supports its creaky structure—which consists of a loose grouping of absurd Keystone Kop situations.

In Klopstockia, since all adults are health addicts and athletes, President Fields decides to enter the country in the Olympics in order to gain back its lost national prestige. Among those participating in the festivities are Jack Oakie, Andy Clyde, Lyda Roberti, Susan

Fleming and Ben Turpin, the popular cross-eyed comic of the silent years. But they all take a back seat to Fields, who arrives to the tune of his own trumpet and drum, asking his cabinet: "Any of you mugs been playing with my harmonica? It's busted."

Klopstockia needs $8,000,000, and Fields comes up with the absurd idea of entering the Olympics as a weight-lifter to help the country out. This scene is hilarious, as Fields skips the first five-hundred-pound weight and—both angered by his opponents and inspired by

MILLION DOLLAR LEGS (1932). With Jack Oakie and Susan Fleming

seductive spy ~~Mata Machree~~ (Lyda Roberti)—gives "the last grunt for his country." Not only does he lift a thousand pound weight, he *throws* it, thus also winning the shot-put event!

Although no one element really dominates this haphazard film, the on-again, off-again subplot involving Mata Machree (who delights in sabotaging the Olympic team's athletic virility with her devastating allure) turns up most often.

In the end, the film—but *not* Fields—seems to run out of steam, although in its brightest moments it is fancy-free and genuinely imaginative. And Fields has a field day debunking the bureaucratic absurdities of governments and international intrigue (although the "spies" constantly popping up do become a bit of a bore). The film is not quite up to the reckless extravagance of *Duck Soup,* but it does tend to prove Fields' notion that a coherent screenplay is not required to put together an entertaining, nonsensical circus—especially if you have a W.C. Fields around as ringmaster.

If I Had a Million starred practically every major performer on the

MILLION DOLLAR LEGS (1932). With Jack Oakie

On the Paramount lot

IF I HAD A MILLION (1932). With Alison Skipworth

Paramount lot: Gary Cooper, George Raft, Charles Laughton, Jack Oakie, Charlie Ruggles, Alison Skipworth, Mary Boland—and W.C. Fields. It was an audience-pleaser, a film of independent episodes bound together by the common theme of a millionaire's gift of money to strangers rather than to his relatives (an idea that must have held a special delight for Fields). The recipients use the money for various purposes, but the Fields section, co-starring Alison Skipworth, was generally considered the high point of a rather uneven movie.

The Fields segment (written by him) was actually a cacophonic symphony of over thirty automobile wrecks. It is somewhat autobiographical, in that Fields had always hated road hogs. Once, while driving his Cadillac, he wrecked his car and put his passenger, Will Rogers, in the hospital. (Fields was trying to overtake a driver who had had the audacity to overtake *him*.) Thus Fields seems to have gotten a personal vengeance—and a good deal of satisfaction—by creating this episode, along with the average harassed motorist who identified gleefully with the Fields segment.

Fields and Skipworth, having saved money all of their lives, buy a new car, only to have it wrecked by an inconsiderate driver as they leave the showroom. Soon after, they are the recipients of a hefty sum of money. They strike upon a scheme of revenge on the world of inconsiderate drivers, and buy a fleet of used cars, helmed by rough, burly types, and take to the road in the forefront of the caravan. As soon as one of those reckless drivers is spotted, the caravan takes after him, not quitting until the unfortunate victim's car is totally demolished.

The episode is slapstick all the way (the car chases and wrecks are funny), but Norman Taurog's direction lacks bite and never achieves the cumulative effect it should have. Nevertheless, the chatter between Fields and Skipworth is inspired enough to make the sequence largely successful, especially for Fields fans. *If I Had a Million* was released by the studio without much fanfare, but it has grown in reputation over the years.

INTERNATIONAL HOUSE (1933). With Peggy Hopkins Joyce and Edmund Breese

INTERNATIONAL HOUSE (1933). With Edmund Breese (left)

Fields appeared next in *International House* (1933). The film somewhat resembles *Million Dollar Legs* in its breezy style and offhand script. International House is a hotel in China (a locale which allows Fields a chance to indulge in several jokes about Orientals, one of his favorite targets*), where representatives from many countries have gathered to observe and bid on the rights to Dr. Wong's new invention, television—here referred to as a "radioscope." Fields, as Professor

Quail, does not have as much to do during the first two-thirds of the film as his fans might have wished; however, he takes over completely during the last section, leaving no doubts as to his commanding comedic presence.

The film's potpourri of talents included vaudeville, musical comedy and radio entertainers. Sharing billing with Rudy Vallee, Bing Crosby, George Burns and Gracie Allen, and Peggy Hopkins Joyce (playing herself), Fields more than held his own. As we see the first shot of him drinking in the cockpit of his small plane, called an autogyro, we hear

* Entangled in the wires of a switchboard, Fields shouts: "It's a Chinese noodle swamp!"

an observer ask: "I wonder if the professor can get off the ground with that load!"

This is followed by a madcap dancing number on the roof garden of the hotel ("she was a China teacup and he was just a mug" is the theme) which is right out of the Busby Berkeley School. In the middle of the party, Fields lands his "Spirit of Brooklyn" on the hotel roof and promptly asks, "Where am I?" Looking quite dapper with his cane and black top hat, he proceeds to make a play for a pretty blonde (Miss Joyce) and has a verbal tumble with the cheerfully dim-witted Gracie Allen (at one point asking, "What's the penalty for murder here?").

The plot premise (international representatives bidding for the new invention) is wisely put aside for the most part, while Fields and Miss Joyce engage in some risqué banter and Burns and Allen interject their familiar routine at various points. In a nutty climactic chase sequence involving Miss Joyce's enraged husband (played by Bela Lugosi), director Edward Sutherland pulls out all the stops.

Some of the lines are quick-witted and funny, with Fields bantering nonstop, mostly about his drinking. Example: Miss Joyce asks him to join her in a glass of wine. Fields responds, "You get in first, and if there's room enough, I'll join you." In another scene, Fields and Miss Joyce, unaware of each other's presence, undress in her suite and go to their separate beds. However, the sound of snoring gives Fields away but he promises the lady he will return, addressing her as "my little calliope."

The TV-invention gimmick is a perfect excuse for introducing several seemingly extraneous musical numbers (although nothing is *really* extraneous to this "plot"), featuring Rudy Vallee (whom Fields insults), Cab Calloway (singing "Have You Ever Met That Reefer Man?") and Baby Rose Marie, later the comedienne Rose Marie of the Dick Van Dyke television show. In the elaborate slapstick finale, Fields takes off in his plane (on his way to Kansas City, he says) with Miss Joyce in the front seat. She soon discovers that she has just sat on a litter of kittens and asks Fields: "I wonder what their parents were?" He replies offhandedly, "Careless, my little cupcake, careless," as they fly off into the clouds.

The success of Fields in *International House* firmed up his bargaining power with Paramount. Although the film itself received generally lukewarm reviews, Fields was universally praised. *Variety* said: "The picture represents Hollywood's mishandling of broad satire, but Fields is permitted to stick mostly to pantomime and he

INTERNATIONAL HOUSE (1933). With Gracie Allen

has a field day." The *New York World Telegram* stated: "The best thing about the picture is the ease and natural wit of Fields, a comic whose appearances on the screen are, regrettably, all too infrequent." And the *Herald-Tribune* noted: "W.C. Fields contributes most of the real humor in his familiar manner, aided by a large cigar and frayed top hat. Watching Mr. Fields in his spectacular car ride through the main lobby is almost worth the price of a ticket."

With these reviews as ammunition, Fields received a long-term contract with the studio, but not without going through a lengthy bargaining session with the top brass. (He mostly whistled and looked out of the window during these sessions, according to those in the know.) In the end, of course, Fields won, getting almost everything (except title approval) he had asked for. During the next six years (1933-1938), he made eleven films for Paramount.

ALICE IN WONDERLAND (1933). As Humpty Dumpty

In his next film, *Alice in Wonderland* (1933), Fields was only one of many performers in a lavish version of the Lewis Carroll classic. Directed by Norman Z. McLeod and designed by William Cameron Menzies, the movie featured a great amount of clever trick photography and was produced with obvious care and a larger-than-usual budget. None of the critics faulted the film's settings or the costumes and makeup for the star-laden cast. What they did carp about, however, was the film's lack of a sense of delight and wonder. The book's special quality had eluded the filmmakers, for the most part, and such favorite players as Gary Cooper (the White Knight), Edna May Oliver (the Red Queen), Jack Oakie (Tweedledum) and Charles Ruggles (the March Hare) were virtually unrecognizable in their elaborate disguises. Fields fans had no doubts, however, as to who was playing the role of Humpty Dumpty. His voice was a dead giveaway, and the absurd Lewis Carroll lines almost seemed to have been written for his delivery. The *Literary Digest*, commenting on the film, noted:

> Even while completely encased in his eggshell, Fields was the only player in the entire cast of stars that was able to create a vivid characterization by his voice alone. This strangely effective voice of his is particularly surprising in view of the fact that he began his theatrical career as a juggler and pantomimist.*

*June 6, 1934.

TILLIE AND GUS (1933). With Clarence Wilson and Alison Skipworth

TILLIE AND GUS (1933). Fields and his card-playing cronies

Tillie and Gus (1933) reunited Alison Skipworth and Fields, and was also Fields' first encounter on screen with Baby LeRoy. Augustus (Fields) and Tillie (Miss Skipworth) made a marvelous team of not-so-honest-but-always-good-hearted ruffians, once married to each other. Long since separated (Gus is a "missionary" in Alaska and Tillie likewise in China), they meet at a railroad ticket office on their way back home to claim an inheritance.

Both gamblers at heart, they don't hesitate to pick up a few extra dollars on the train in a fast poker game. Fields exclaims about one of his partners: "Crooked as a dog's hind leg." He plays stupid at first ("Pinochle—that's the top of something, isn't it?") but with Tillie standing nearby signaling ("I'll credit your share of this to the alimony account," she says later), he can't help but cheat honest but gullible men.

When they arrive in Seattle, they discover that their niece and her husband and child (Baby LeRoy) are being swindled out of a ferry-boat franchise by a man named Phineas Pratt (Clarence Wilson). Fields seizes up the chance to beat Pratt at his own game, and challenges him to a boat race. He takes over as captain of an old ferry to win the race in a rousing conclusion, although along the way Fields almost loses Baby LeRoy to the river. (His bathtub slides overboard.)

The two old-timers, Tillie and Gus, make an endearing couple

MISSISSIPPI (1935). With Bing Crosby

—and Fields and Skipworth play them to the hilt. The ferry-boat race is energetic and delightful, and Fields plays the part of a would-be sea captain with obvious relish. He also gets the chance to utter some pointedly funny lines. Asked by Tillie whether he likes children, he answers: "I do, if they're properly cooked." Later, he describes his ex-wife Tillie as being "as solid as a brick telephone booth," and after winning the race and being told by his niece's husband that it was "the world's greatest gamble," Fields answers: "Don't forget, Lady Godiva put everything she had on a horse!"

The movie's tone is both irreverent and heartwarming, an incongruous combination which somehow works charmingly here, although some Fields fans thought it much too gentle and subdued for the freewheeling pre-Code year of 1933.

Mississippi (1935) greatly resembles *Tillie and Gus* in its tone and easygoing humor. Fields shared co-starring billing with Bing Crosby, and they were supported by Joan Bennett, Gail Patrick and Queenie Smith. The film, directed by Edward Sutherland, contained lovely, if rather synthetic, touches in its setting of a magnolia-and-mint-julep Old South. (It was based on Booth Tarkington's novel, *Magnolia.*) Unfortunately, Fields' part as a showboat skipper was not the

MISSISSIPPI (1935). With Jean Rouverol, Mildred Stone, Mary Ellen Brown, and Mabel Van Buren

SIX OF A KIND (1934). With Gracie Allen, Mary Boland, and George Burns

center of the story—most of the movie was built around Crosby's romances and his crooning of several Rodgers and Hart songs (including "Easy to Remember"). The plot satirizes the Southern code of honor—Crosby refuses to engage in a duel precipitated by a trivial matter, thus losing his fiancée but later winning her sister. Most of the Fields humor was verbal (some of it throwaway gags), although there is a hilarious poker game (much like the one in *Poppy*) that must be seen to be believed—he winds up with *five* aces!

Fields tells several tall Indian tales (Question: "How long have you been navigating the river?" Answer: "Ever since I took it away from the Indians."), and makes his often-quoted statement on marriage: "It's o.k. for women. Women are like elephants to me—I like to look at 'em, but I wouldn't want to own one." He also introduces his famous expletive, "Mother-of-Pearl!"

After taking Crosby aboard his showboat and turning him into a legendary (but untried) dead shot, (Fields tells him: "You stick to me,

70

I'll have you hunting bears with a flyswatter"), he gives the "Singing Killer," as Crosby is labeled, some sound advice: "A dead fish can float downstream, but it takes a live fish to swim up." As the film comes to a close, with Crosby and Miss Bennett in a clinch, Fields murmurs laughingly: "Some of my best friends are Indians—shot Indians!"

In 1934, Fields made Six of a Kind and Mrs. Wiggs of the Cabbage Patch, appearing in supporting roles in both films. The former, directed by expert comedy craftsman Leo McCarey, included Charlie Ruggles, Mary Boland, Alison Skipworth and Burns and Allen. The thin plot concerns Ruggles and wife Boland traveling by car to the West Coast. They take on the oddball couple of Burns and Allen, plus their enormous Great Dane, as traveling companions. Unwittingly, Ruggles is carrying a briefcase containing $50,000 in stolen bank money, placed there by a fellow employee who had intended to rob them on the road. Fields, as Sheriff John Hoxley, and his partner in law enforcement, Mrs. K. Rumford, the local innkeeper (Alison Skipworth again) are tipped off to the stolen money and apprehend the foursome when they reach their Nevada town. The apprehension and arrest, of the "culprits", appearing toward the end, is probably the funniest scene in the film.

Fields tackles his part with gusto, probably pleased by the irony of his playing a sheriff. He even works in a game of billiards, while describing how he came to be called "Honest John." (He also remarks that everything really pleasant "is either illegal, immoral, or fattening.") Despite his limited footage, Fields embellished Six of a Kind with a hearty dose of much-needed nonsensical comedy.

Mrs. Wiggs of the Cabbage Patch is a strangely sentimental romanticization of poverty which top-lined Pauline Lord as Mrs. Wiggs. The film, directed by Norman Taurog, is a warm and charming version of the popular old novel and play (filmed before in 1914 and 1919, and then later in 1942), but Fields-followers were probably champing at the bit, since he does not appear until the last twenty minutes. Fields is Mr. Stubbins, the mail-order husband of neighbor ZaSu Pitts, a decidedly minor role for the comedian. Although his small-talk with Miss Pitts (as she cooks him an elaborate dinner) is amusing, the fact that he is given very little to do (no pool, juggling or child-baiting) did not please his disappointed audiences.

But Fields made up for this glaring omission in his remaining 1934 films, You're Telling Me, It's a Gift, and The Old-Fashioned Way. The first was a remake of Fields' silent film So's Your Old Man, with only a

SIX OF A KIND (1934). With Gracie Allen, George Burns, Charlie Ruggles, and Mary Boland

MRS. WIGGS OF THE CABBAGE PATCH (1934). With ZaSu Pitts and Pauline Lord

YOU'RE TELLING ME (1934). Fields is detained for leading an ostrich.

few minor changes in the basic storyline. (The shatterproof glass invention is changed to puncture-proof rubber tires.) Fields was especially at home playing the disreputable inventor of mad devices, the town reprobate who finally achieves success. He is again the henpecked husband with a less-than-warm wife. At one point, his wife (Louise Carter) is told by a neighbor, "I think you're the luckiest woman in the world," and she replies swiftly, "Why, is my husband dead?"

Audiences found the film most satisfying and delightful—and perhaps only Fields could make a scene such as an attempted suicide magically hilarious. (He finds better and better reasons for not taking the poison.) He also performed his by-now celebrated golf game. Sam Brisbee served as a model for many of Fields' succeeding roles—it is almost a monologue demonstrating the comedian's special style and wit, the philosophy of which might be summed up best by one of Fields' comments to his two old drinking buddies: "It's a funny old world—a man's lucky if he gets out of it alive." No viewer could ever forget the crazy scene which has Fields leading a giant ostrich on a rope down the street. (A friend had suggested he take a bird home to his wife as a pet to assuage her ruffled feathers.) He finally gives the rope to a friend, saying: "Hold the chickadee—if she starts singing —give her some birdseed."

It's a Gift was certainly one of the best feature films Fields made during his Paramount years. The film, drawing on elements of two silent movies, *The Potters* and *It's the Old Army Game* (plus material written by Fields under the name of Charles Bogle), is atypical in that Fields' Harold Bissonette, a rags-to-riches character in a basically downtrodden family, doesn't seem to have an ounce (or maybe just a half ounce) of malevolence in his body.

Fields owns a small-town general store and is badgered by his wife, customers and relatives. Out of desperation, he buys an orange ranch through the mail, and takes the wife, daughter and her fiancé across the country to the property, as they protest all the way (the money for

YOU'RE TELLING ME (Paramount, 1934). Alfred Delcambre, Joan Marsh, Larry "Buster" Crabbe, Louise Carter, W.C. Fields, Adrienne Ames

IT'S A GIFT (1934). As Harold Bissonette

IT'S A GIFT (1934). With Jean Rouverol, Kathleen Howard and Tommy Bupp

the trip and the ranch having been provided by an inheritance). When they arrive, they discover that the property, a parched stretch of land, is worthless as an orange grove, although promoters want the land to build a race track. Fields shrewdly holds out for a fantastic sum (his wife thinks he's crazy)—$40,000 and the chance to settle down on a *real* orange grove.

Some critics took special note of a scene in Fields' general store in-

volving a blind and deaf old man who played a kind of comic villain. The man (Charles Sellon) practically destroys Fields' store—plate glass windows, light bulbs, even a display of kumquats, and then walks out into the street, narrowly missing cars in the heavy traffic as the flabbergasted Fields looks on. It was a joke which could have backfired into a dreadful lapse of taste; instead, it comes off as masterly comedy.

Fields also has several maddening encounters on the porch where he is trying to get some sleep but is constantly interrupted. A mysterious man turns up, looking for a "Karl La Fong." Most annoying, however, is Baby LeRoy, who insists on squeezing grapes from above, causing the juice to fall onto Fields' head. ("Shades of Bacchus!," he shouts at little LeRoy.) In another scene, the boy removes a cork from a large barrel of molasses, forcing Fields to put up a sign on his front door: "Closed on account of molasses."

It has been widely reported that Fields, somewhat miffed and maybe even jealous at Baby LeRoy's scene-stealing tactics, got the child drunk on the set by spiking his orange juice. When LeRoy was unable to work for the rest of the day, a delighted Fields remarked: "The kid's no trouper—send him home!"

IT'S A GIFT (1934). With Kathleen Howard

THE OLD-FASHIONED WAY (1934). The Great McGonigle plies his wares.

Critics complained about the movie's fairly shoddy production values and less-than-first-rate photography, but most agreed that it was an astonishing tour de force for Fields, who must have privately enjoyed the film's lovely ending: his wife and children enter a chauffeur-driven limousine, as Fields, all smiles, privately enjoys a tall drink.

In *The Old-Fashioned Way*, (again from an original story by Charles Bogle/alias Fields), Fields is back to his old self—and he gets back at Baby LeRoy for the child's pranks in *It's a Gift* by kicking him on the seat of his pants. As a crooked actor-manager known as The Great McGonigle (a role he was to repeat in *Poppy* in 1936), Fields goes all out to camouflage his essential selfishness and dishonesty by wearing rather florid period costumes and exaggerating his comic gestures somewhat more than usual.

Always one step ahead of the law, McGonigle leads his turn-of-the-century troupe of thespians across the country, offering a production of *The Drunkard*, which is performed during the movie's final section with Fields playing the nasty Squire Cribbs. Fields is constantly eluding irate sheriffs and is supported by a loving daughter (a role, played here by Judith Allen, that was to reappear in several of his later films). *The Old-Fashioned Way* is laced with gags and bits of characterization that would turn up throughout Fields' remaining films, to the delight of his loyal fans.

McGonigle's arrivals in town are obviously special "occasions," complete with band music and cordial greetings by local dignitaries, who are unaware that Fields has already prepared a "sucker list" of prime candidates for his prey. In one such town, Fields and his troupe are ensconced in Mrs. Wendelschaffer's boarding house where he is introduced to Cleopatra Pepperday (Jan Duggan), a rich and frustrated singer to whom he dangles the possibility of a stage part and maybe even marriage. (To her face he calls her his little "Rocky Mountain Canary," but aside she's really his "Rocky Mountain Goat.") She also has a little son, Baby LeRoy, who splatters Fields with food, dips his watch in molasses and twists his nose. This byplay winds up with the famous boot in the rear by an unamused Fields.

The actual production of *The Drunkard* is highly stylized, with Fields playing the villain in a large black hat and even getting a chance to intone, "It ain't a fit night out for man nor beast!" Fields juggles, there's a musical number, and the whole thing is a laughable satire on the "home sweet home" theme. Throughout this sequence, Fields seems to be taking particular pleasure in playing the role to the hilt —brandishing his cane or foul-looking cigar and wearing odd-looking medicine-show clothes. The slapstick plot of *The Drunkard* is almost an afterthought, and the scene itself might be best remembered as most legitimately recording Fields' full vaudeville act, performed in close shots with little or no cutaways. The performance ends with Fields receiving a tomato in the face, hurled by none other than Baby LeRoy.

The film could have ended on a note of pathos, but it doesn't, of course. Fields accepts a job as master-of-ceremonies of a medicine show (decidedly lower down on the "show-biz" professional rung), while pretending to desert his daughter, who will marry happily. This is reminiscent of *Sally of the Sawdust*, but *The Old-Fashioned Way* ends on a more uproarious note as Fields and a pal outwit the

THE OLD-FASHIONED WAY (1934). With Jan Duggan

MAN ON THE FLYING TRAPEZE (1935). With Oscar Apfel and Lew Kelly

landlady, chiseling her out of the rent. In the end, Fields says: "Isn't it wonderful, how everything rounds itself out, eventually," and most audiences were inclined to agree.

In *Man on the Flying Trapeze* (1935), again based on an original story by Fields using the alias of Charles Bogle, the comedian creates another domestic role—this time as Ambrose Wolfinger, an of-fice worker (whose amazing filing system defies understanding), a henpecked husband (he prefers drinking applejack in his cellar with burglars to sleeping with his wife) and a loving father (his daughter by a first marriage adores him.)

Considering his shrewish wife (Kathleen Howard), nitpicking mother-in-law (Vera Lewis) and slothful brother-in-law Claude

MAN ON THE FLYING TRAPEZE (1935). With Vera Lewis, Joe Sawyer, and James Burke

(Grady Sutton), it's no wonder that Fields gets drunk with the burglars and winds up in jail. At work, he asks for his first day off in twenty-five years to go to a wrestling match, telling his boss he must attend his mother-in-law's funeral. ("It's hard to lose a mother-in-law," the boss remarks. "Yes, it is," Fields replies. "Very hard. Almost impossible.") At the film's conclusion, however, all ends well, as Fields gets a raise and punches his lazy brother-in-law in the face.

His role and the film itself are classic Fields—the plot is easy to take, the dialogue has many great Fields one-liners, and his masterly delivery enhances even the weak material. As with most Fields films, the production was most unpretentious, possibly adding to the audience's ability to identify readily with this family man who has been oppressed by the world and harassed by the weight of odious domesticity, while maintaining a courageous semblance of dignity.

In addition to Fields' use of the slang term "Oh, drat!," the picture is also noteworthy for several other reasons: the appearance of Fields' off-screen romance Carlotta Monti in the small role of his loyal, adoring secretary (they would live together for over a dozen years, first at his rented Bel Air mansion and later in a large house on De Mille Drive); Fields' naming the shiftless bro-ther-in-law "Claude," which was, in fact, the name of his own son (at this point, he had long been estranged from his wife and son); Fields' incisive digs at the American system of legal "justice," as Ambrose, handcuffed, pleads before a judge who has just fined him $30 or thirty days for not having a license to manufacture applejack, while the two criminals are set free; and the special satisfaction (both personal and professional) Fields must have received in writing the film's final scene: Ambrose Wolfinger, driving a big new car with drink in hand and daughter and wife in the front seat, is seen casting satisfactory glances at the rumble seat where mother-in-law and brother-in-law are ensconced—as the rains pour down!

After *Man on the Flying Trapeze,* Fields made *David Copperfield* for MGM in 1935. He was to make only two more films for Paramount, *Poppy* in 1936 and *The Big Broadcast of 1938. Poppy* was, of course, a re-creation of Fields' successful Broadway role and a remake of the 1925 silent film, *Sally of the Sawdust.* In his review of the film, Graham Greene said the following:

Fields wins our hearts not by a display of Chaplin sentiment, not by class solidarity (he robs the poor as promptly as the rich), but simply by the completeness of his dishonesty. To watch Mr. Fields, as Dickensian

83

as anything Dickens ever wrote, is a form of escape for poor human creatures.*

*Graham Greene, *Graham Greene on Film* Simon and Schuster (New York, 1972), p. 88.

Fields was very ill before and immediately after the shooting of *Poppy,* and many of his scenes were done by a double. Nevertheless, what we do see of him does not indicate that he was especially sick. The

POPPY (1936). With Catherine Doucet

POPPY (1936).
With Rosalind Keith

THE BIG BROADCAST OF 1938 (1938). A crisis aboard the steamship Gigantic

film itself is not nearly as good as the silent version; the latter was less complicated and more heartfelt. And, ironically, the silent version played much more realistically, since it had been shot by Griffith in an actual New England setting, while director Edward Sutherland filmed *Poppy* entirely on the Hollywood back lot. What we do remember about *Poppy*, however, is the vision of Fields with his white stovepipe hat, spats, cutaway coat and cane pulling off the sale of a so-called "talking dog" to a customer who could only be described, in Fields' word, as a "sucker," and McGargle's parting advice to his daughter (rather woodenly played by Rochelle Hudson): "Never give a sucker an even break."

Fields' last Paramount film, *The Big Broadcast of 1938*, was one in which he played a supporting role. It was not really his sort of movie, being a rambling musical extravaganza studded with foolish subplots. Probably improvising his routines, Fields played a dual role: T. Frothingwell Bellows, millionaire playboy, and his less extravagant brother, S.B. Bellows. The story revolves around a transatlantic race between two massive ocean liners and features some generally entertaining, though rather inane musical numbers, performed by Martha Raye (as T.F. Bellows' zany daughter), Dorothy Lamour, Bob Hope, and opera star Kirsten Flagstad, among others.

Early in the movie, Fields is given an opportunity to do part of his golf routine, but once the plot hops aboard the ocean liners, it turns decidedly romantic—leaving room for only sporadic appearances by Fields, who does brief but familiar routines, including a variation of his pool act. He had suggested a number of revisions in his part, but unfortunately none were adopted. As his swan song to a studio for which he had worked the better part of the decade, Fields himself might have sung the film's leading song, "Thanks for the Memory." Instead, Bob Hope, joined by Shirley Ross, did the honors in his first full-length feature role.

Fields had always admired Charles Dickens—and when the role of Mr. Micawber came up, he convinced the MGM brass that he—and only he—could do it justice. And he did. Producer David Selznick (who had first offered the role to Charles Laughton, who turned it down) and director George Cukor had some reservations about whether Fields would fit his Dickensian costume properly, not only literally, but also figuratively. (Perhaps they worried whether he might try to slip in a juggling routine at some point.) Even though the role required more "straight" dramatic acting than usual for Fields, Mr. Micawber was a character with whom Fields' audiences—even those not especially fond of Charles Dickens—could identify. It was temperamentally suited to the Fieldsian model—the mildly dishonest, somewhat henpecked but essentially likable man merely trying to keep one step ahead of his creditors and his boss.

Fields' total screen time in *David Copperfield* was just under a half hour. He appeared in only four major scenes, each occuring during a different time period in the story. He was, nevertheless, a unifying character, and one whose presence was essential to sustaining a sense of continuity in the narrative line.

Micawber's first appearance in the film is memorable and entirely

BETWEEN STUDIOS: MGM, RADIO, AND ILLNESS

appropriate, as he enters the Micawber cottage via the rooftops and through a window (as usual, his creditors are at hand), as if a spirit of great jocularity were descending from the heavens wearing top hat, spats and carrying a cane. Fields carries himself as Micawber in an altogether roguish and charming manner, and it is immediately apparent that his wonderfully realized screen presence makes everyone around him bloom.

Micawber borrows some money from young David (Freddie Bartholomew) and assures him that although he is being hounded by creditors, "I am confidently expecting something to turn up." Unfortunately, he is served with a court order for debt while walking with David, and he sighs, "I am forever flawed." David later visits him in prison, their last time together until they meet some years later at Mr. Wickfield's house.

David (now Frank Lawton) has grown up and become a writer. He meets Mr. Micawber, who is employed at the Wickfield residence, and again lends his old friend some money. Micawber tells David he has been offered a job by Uriah

88

DAVID COPPERFIELD (1935). With Freddie Bartholomew

DAVID COPPERFIELD (1935). With the Micawber children, Mrs. Micawber (Jean Cadell), David (Freddie Bartholomew), and Clickett (Elsa Lanchester)

Heep (Roland Young) and intends to take it. They meet sometime later, and Micawber does a devastating takeoff on his "'umble" but sneaky employer whom he has grown to dislike intensely. (He tells David that he has given Heep a heap of I.O.U.s.)

Fields' finale is his best and most dramatically effective scene in the film. He turns on the crafty Heep,

revealing him as a swindler and fraud. Heep begins to strike back, but Micawber retaliates marvelously, shouting, "Approach me, you heap of infamy!" as he acts out a mock swordfight with his cane. The part obviously warmed Fields' heart, and it is to MGM's credit that they eventually cast him in the role, even though Fields admittedly gave the top brass (including Samuel

DAVID COPPERFIELD (1935). With Freddie Bartholomew

DAVID COPPERFIELD (1935). With Freddie Bartholomew

Goldwyn himself) a bit of trouble by staging a no-work strike halfway through the shooting in order to effect higher wages. As usual, Fields won.

In 1936, Fields spent some months at Seboba Hot Springs and at the Riverside Hospital, resting from a severe illness not unrelated to the enormous amount of alcohol (two quarts a day) he was now consuming. Fields claimed that alcohol acted as a sedative for his strung-out nerves, and that it whetted his sense of humor. He was almost never seen in a drunken state, however; in fact, he despised drunks. After the shooting of *Poppy* in 1936, Fields developed a critical case of pneumonia and other complications. Many of his friends thought he would die, and his recovery was a slow one. But when he did recover, he emerged from his sickbed to greet his startled admirers with the comment: "Oh, ye of little faith."

Even Fields probably realized at this point that his long addiction to alcohol had taken its toll, although he himself would never make that admission publicly. Reportedly he went on the wagon for several months, but soon was back to his usual 2 quarts a day. (His friends made vain attempts to water down the liquor.) At one point, when his doctor told him to give up drinking, if he wanted to live more than a month, Fields replied: "You must be a good doctor. That's what the specialist in Berlin told me twenty-five years ago." He spent the rest of 1937 in a sanitarium, regaining what he could of his shattered health.

Having withdrawn from films temporarily, Fields entered a new —albeit brief—career in radio, a medium with which he was soon to become bored and even scornful. ("They might as well put a ventriloquist's dummy on there as a juggler," he once stated.) Nevertheless, the 1937-38 radio audience was probably the largest audience he attracted in his entire career.

Even in the early thirties, many radio producers had tried in vain to cajole Fields to star in his own radio show. During his convalescence of 1936-37, Fields discovered that he could easily do radio programs from his sickbed. His voice was heard for the first time over radio in a program honoring Paramount's Adolph Zukor.

But for the short time he worked steadily in radio, Fields delighted audiences and was a big hit. A CBS press release, obviously ecstatic to have snatched Fields for a guest appearance on its "Your Hit Parade" show, stated:

> To try and capture the flavor of W.C. Fields on the printed page is an effrontery, and the numbing record of this master trouper gives little hint of the subtle magic of his mimicry, the jaunty pomposity of his transparent villainy, the artful blend of warmhearted chicanery and injured innocence which have won him the acclaim of an international audience around the world.

Fields might have had a quiet laugh himself at the overblown pomposity of the press release. Nevertheless, it does indicate the degree of enthusiasm with which the radio networks welcomed this master comedian whose voice had done so much to make him a household name.

Fields loved ribbing his sponsor's products. (While doing his own show for Lucky Strike cigarettes, he would constantly refer to his son, "Chester Field.") As was to be expected, he ad-libbed a good deal of the material, which worked best with his newfound partners Edgar Bergen and his impudent, roguish puppet-friend Charlie McCarthy, with whom Fields developed a running feud on the "Chase & Sanborn Hour." This "feud" was carried right over into Fields' first Universal film in 1939, *You Can't Cheat an Honest Man.* He would refer to Charlie as "a flophouse for termites," "a woodpecker's snack bar," or "a belligerent little bundling board," while the dummy retorted: "Why you two-legged martini, you weren't born, you were squeezed out of a bar rag."

Chase & Sanborn paid Fields $6,500 a week, and later Lucky Strike raised that to $7,500. Fields, however, was unsatisfied being on radio only, and took out a full-page ad in *The Hollywood Reporter* to announce that he was ready to give his fans not only his voice, but also the chance to once again see him on screen. Universal soon heeded his call; nevertheless, interspersed with his film commitments, Fields continued doing sporadic radio appearances until 1943.

On radio in 1937

At age sixty, Fields came into his own as a film comedian. He made a splendid deal with Universal (a much more informal studio than Paramount) which allowed him to demand and get his own way. The four films he made for Universal between 1938 and 1941, *You Can't Cheat an Honest Man, The Bank Dick, My Little Chickadee* and *Never Give a Sucker an Even Break,* were all written by Fields (except for *My Little Chickadee,* which was co-authored by Mae West), and along with the four Mack Sennett two-reelers and *It's a Gift, The Old-Fashioned Way* and *Man on the Flying Trapeze* (all authored by Fields under the name of Charles Bogle) they were his most persuasive works. Whether what Fields wrote were "stories," "treatments" or "ideas," or were scribbled on the backs of laundry tickets or grocery bills, he demanded and received screen credit from Universal (under such preposterous names as Mahatma Kane Jeeves and Otis Criblecoblis) and a financial reward of as much as $25,000, in addition to his regular salary of $125,000 per movie. The films were not as expensively produced as some he had done for Paramount, but Fields' brand of cinematic comedy did not need money as one of its prerequisites.

Fields ad-libbed much of his dialogue—even more than he had

THE UNIVERSAL YEARS: A SUSTAINED HIGH

previously—in his four Universal films. He once said to his secretary: "I ad-lib most of my dialogue. If I did remember my lines, it would be too bad for me." *You Can't Cheat an Honest Man* (1939) was a romp for Fields and his supporting players, Edgar Bergen and his two cohorts, Charlie McCarthy and Mortimer Snerd. The film itself is ramshackle and shapeless but also very funny. The star, let loose again in a circus atmosphere, was in top form, drinking, swindling, circus-barking*—even dabbling a bit in ventriloquism. This was the only one of the four Universal Films to be directed by George Marshall; the other three were helmed by Edward Cline. Fields took credit for the original story, again using the name of Charles Bogle, a character from *You're Telling Me.*

As circus owner Larson E. Whipsnade, Fields is constantly being chased by local sheriffs over failure to pay his bills and he can't get rid of Bergen and McCarthy because of their contract. There's a romantic

*Barker Fields introduces two seemingly ordinary men to his audience: "Two brothers who baffle science. Side by side—the world's smallest giant and the world's largest midget!"

YOU CAN'T CHEAT AN HONEST MAN (1939). With Constance Moore

'YOU CAN'T CHEAT AN HONEST MAN (1939). Fields' snake stories causes
Mrs. Bel-Goodie (Mary Forbes) to faint.

*YOU CAN'T CHEAT AN HONEST MAN (1939). With Thurston Hall,
James Bush, and John Arledge*

subplot (Bergen falls in love with
Whipsnade's daughter Vicky,
played by Constance Moore), but
Vicky decides that "true love" will
have to take a back seat to improv-
ing her father's financial affairs. She
accepts the marriage proposal of
Roger Bel-Goodie (James Bush), a
rich suitor, as Fields advises her:
"Getting married is like going into a
strange saloon."

There's a madcap moment when
Bergen and McCarthy are sent up
in a balloon, only to spot Vicky on
her way to the marriage ceremony.
They jump out, land on her car
—and all three wind up at the local
police station. Meanwhile Whipsnade entertains himself at the Bel-
Goodie estate (in a scene reminiscent of the one in *Her Majesty,
Love*), arriving in a chariot. He enters the mansion, tips the butler
who asks for his card, and responds,
"I don't need a card, son. Where's
the bar?" (Fields hated pretentious
American social values, such as the
calling card, and enjoyed satirizing

YOU CAN'T CHEAT AN HONEST MAN (1939). Fields disguised as "Buffalo Bella"

them at every opportunity.)

Fields tells some tall tales about rattlesnakes to his hostess, who naturally has a morbid fear of snakes. She faints dead away at several points in his narrative, prompting the astonished Fields to say: "Why, some of my best friends are snakes." Before leaving the house, Fields plays a wild game of ping-pong with a mysterious, chain-smoking society lady (she asks him "how's your ping-pong?" and he responds, "fine, how's yours?"). Daughter Vicky finally arrives, and realizing what has happened, tells off her no-longer-prospective-mother-in-law: "Why don't you get off the trapeze and come down into the sawdust where you belong?" They leave, and the picture trails off as the troupe heads for the nearest state line. In a final shot, we see Mortimer Snerd in a balloon commenting on the goings-on from above: "It's a great race, folks. Glad I'm safe up here."

There is a curious makeshift quality about the film, although it is well-paced and certainly Fields' best work since 1935. Fields' Larson Whipsnade, the circus proprietor, is *not* as lovable a fraud as many of the roles he'd created. And his feud with Charlie McCarthy seems to go on much too long. (This, of course, is a continuation of their famous radio feud, which had Fields bellowing such lines as "Charlie, I'll throw a woodpecker on you.")

But who can forget the insane happenings: Fields taking a shower in a portable shower bath of his own invention (an elephant named Queenie sprays warm water from her trunk); Fields' attempt to hide from the sheriff, disguising himself as "Buffalo Bella," the bearded lady and shooting champ, and many other moments of inspired lunacy. Fields is entertaining throughout, at one point imitating Edgar Bergen by performing a very funny ventriloquist routine and later screaming to his daughter, "Who took the cork out of my lunch?"

Universal's signing of both Mae West and W. C. Fields as co-stars of *My Little Chickadee* (1940) was a major coup and turned out to be the most profitable of the four starring vehicles Fields did for Universal. Miss West's movie career had passed its peak in the mid-thirties (the Production Code had clamped down heavily on her risqué material), and Fields was pleased at the prospect of this unique comedy team. Mae (Flower Belle Lee), hip-swinging, eye-rolling and murmuring her double entendres in that nasal, insinuating voice, hit the Western trail with Fields, who played Cuthbert J. Twillie, a penniless hair-oil salesman and her willing but ignored husband of convenience. Mae's real eye is for a romantic masked bandit with whom

MY LITTLE CHICKADEE (1940). With Mae West

MY LITTLE CHICKADEE (1940). With Margaret Hamilton

MY LITTLE CHICKADEE (1940). Twillie gives Flower Belle an admiring look.

she has a rendezvous one night after substituting a goat for herself in bed with Cuthbert. (Discovering his strange plight, Fields shouts "Godfrey Daniel!")

Never one to miss an opportunity to advance her station in life, Flower Belle has married Cuthbert only because she is convinced he is loaded (with money). The union is also a way of appeasing local gossips (especially one Mrs. Gideon, played by the unfailingly marvelous Margaret Hamilton) who feel that an unattached Flower Belle is too dire a threat to their menfolk's sense of monogamy.

The storyline of this burlesque fable of the gamy Wild West of the eighties is thin if not emaciated. There is the usual amount of Old West gun-slinging, horse-riding, and bandit-baiting, all indifferently handled, but what makes the movie interesting is the almost cat-and-mouse manner in which Miss West and Fields alternate their routines. (She has a skit as a schoolteacher who teaches the children a few facts not in their books—he plays cards and relates tall tales to saloon customers.)

At the time of the film's shooting, there was industry gossip that director Edward Cline would probably spend most of his time acting as referee between his two stars. This may or may not have happened (various biographers give differing accounts), but based on what appears on screen, it would seem that the fireworks were kept to a low level. Miss West's material (which she wrote) is all recognizably Westian, and for the most part, she plays it well; the same is true of Fields. But their comedy styles are so different that there is really no valid critical comparison between the two. Mae's routines are carefully polished, while Fields' are the usual combination of improvisation, ad-libbing, and outrageously memorable lines. (Sample: he is playing cards with an Indian, who asks, "Is this a game of chance?" and Fields replies, "Not the way I play it.")

The movie looks as if it were edited by a mathematician who allowed an equal amount of footage to each star. And perhaps the expected clashing of the two stars did not fully materialize because their scenes together are kept to a miminum. The few times they are seen together are memorable, as in their first meeting on a train. Cuthbert kisses Flower Belle's hand, exclaiming, "What symmetrical digits!," then presents his card to her stating: "Cuthbert J. Twillie —Novelties and Notions" as she wisecracks, "What kinda notions ya got?" He asks her to tell him something about herself. Flower Belle says that she can't tell him anything good. "I can see what's good," Twillie replies. "Tell me the rest."

MY LITTLE CHICKADEE (1940). A classic encounter. In the middle:
Harlan Briggs

THE BANK DICK (1940). With Una Merkel

THE BANK DICK (1940). Fields expresses his feelings about children.

Another joint highlight is their so-called "bedroom" scene, with Fields an anxious bridegroom to West's reluctant bride. Locked outside the room, Fields looks through the keyhole and bellows, "My dear, I have some definite pear-shaped ideas to discuss with you."

Fields' solo scenes are also delightful. At one point, attending a testimonial dinner celebrating his elevation to sheriff by the grateful townsfolk, Fields sits at the end of a long banquet table where he becomes entangled with a falling parasol and feathers which float into his soup. In another scene, Fields, as combination sheriff and bartender, engages in banter in the saloon, shamelessly relating tall tales and white lies and reminiscing about having tended bar on lower East Broadway!

Probably the closest each star gets to parodying the other is when Mae kisses a masked Cuthbert and immediately recognizes that inimitable nose; and the last scene in the movie where Fields does a takeoff on Miss West's "Why-don't-you-come-up-and-see-me?" routine. A helter-skelter but uproarious film, *My Little Chickadee* is one of those comedies whose sum of its parts is better than the whole.

The Bank Dick (1940) may have been one of Fields' more perfectly realized film scripts, and was certainly the apex of his career in movies. Not only does the film burlesque the hypocrisy of small-town middle-American morals, it also mocks the notion of finding real happiness through newfound wealth. Fields wrote it under the name Mahatma Kane Jeeves (the project was known to be his special pet at the studio, and they gave him completely free reign), and as in *It's a Gift*, he's the henpecked father of one of those hilariously awful families. The plot, a direct assult on the Protestant work ethic, finds Fields, the town drunk, and his sniveling son-in-law-to-be (Grady Sutton) embezzling funds from a local bank in order to invest the money in stocks for a beefsteak mine. In this post-Watergate era, the logic seems to hit home: success through stealing is perfectly acceptable as long as you're lucky enough *not* to get caught.

The film is often illogical, frequently irreverent, and always wildly farcical. There's a marvelous quality of planned anarchy, if such a contradiction is possible. *The Bank Dick*'s moral theme may have shocked some viewers, but others insisted that Fields was just reflecting society—that going along with corruption without complaining was engaging in a kind of nationwide conformity. Of course, Fields elevates this feeling to an art and raises the ante by insisting on doing the thieving himself. Whether he

THE BANK DICK (1940). With Franklin Pangborn

achieves "respectablity" or not —and he does in *The Bank Dick*—the pure-chance aspects of life are so wonderfully illuminated in the film that audiences could not help but identify with protagonist Egbert Sousé.

The very idea that Fields, as Sousé, would be called in to "pinch-hit" as movie director for a film company shooting in his town (the actual director, one A. Pismo Clam, is drunk) is, in itself, inspired. Things get back to normal when the director sobers up, and Sousé returns to his usual routine —waiting for the Black Pussy Café to open. (How that not-so-subtle "obscenity" escaped the censors' scissors is a real mystery.) While simply minding his own affairs, Sousé is mistakenly credited with "capturing" an escaping bank robber. (Actually all he does is stick out his feet for the robber to trip over.) Now a local "hero," Sousé is given a respectable job—a position at the local bank—as a reward.

The plot takes a turn for the bizarre when Fields agrees to buy some shares of stock—that is, he convinces his prospective son-in-law Og Oggilby to do so, thinking that the added income will enable Og to have a large enough nest egg to marry his daughter. Og, a teller at the bank, temporarily "borrows" the funds for the transaction, intending to replace them shortly.

Unfortunately, a prissy bank inspector, J. Pinkerton Snoopington (Franklin Pangborn), arrives unexpectedly, and Sousé attempts unsuccessfully to stall the examination by getting him soused at the local cafe on "Michael Finns."

In a truly crazy resolution to the tale, Sousé becomes the "hero" of a second bank robbery—again, unwittingly—and is rewarded to the tune of five thousand dollars for capturing the bandit in a wild chase and ten thousand dollars for the story he sells to the movies. (Universal must have swallowed hard at this one.) With his money problems solved, Sousé now spends even more time at the local café in an ending which exudes both warmth and a kind of strange melancholy.

The Bank Dick takes off not only on banks and our system of morality and justice, but also on the movie industry itself. At one point, Fields tells a wide-eyed local audience, "In the old days, I used to outdrink Keaton, Chaplin, Arbuckle . . . I can't get celluloid out of my blood." The film's Keystone comedy elements are also undeniable. (Cline had directed several during the heyday of their popularity.) But what really makes *The Bank Dick* such a satisfying film is the fact that it is a one-man show backed up by an excellent group of sharply professional comedy performers. (As Sousé's nasty wife and mother-in-

NEVER GIVE A SUCKER AN EVEN BREAK (1941). With Leon Errol

law, Cora Witherspoon and Jessie Ralph are peerless.)

Never Give a Sucker an Even Break (1941) is a horse of a different color. It was the most absurd and completely Fieldsian of his four Universal movies, with a structure sometimes incoherent and usually incredible. There is almost no "plot" in the conventional sense of the word; instead, Fields draws a bead on movie plots by reducing the film to a satire of the movie industry itself. The film's form is its very formlessness.

Fields wanted to call the movie *The Great Man*. When the studio chose the present title, legend has it that Fields growled: "What does it matter? They can't get that on a marquee. It will probably boil down to 'Fields—Sucker.' " (The title is, of course, the line most often associated with Fields—but it was not his invention, whether or not it was his philosophy. It is generally recognized as a line by Wilson Mizner, introduced by Fields to the public in the 1923 stage version of *Poppy*.) The story most often told about the film's original inception is that Fields wrote the script (under the pen name of Otis Criblecoblis) on the back of an envelope or grocery bill while sitting on the toilet. The story may very well be false; the spirit in which it is told, however, is a perfectly accurate reflection of the spirit of the movie. *Never Give a Sucker an Even Break* was attacked at the time of its release as being too thin and bizarre, but some critics have now included it on their lists of all-time best films.

If the movie's plotline can be condensed, this is it: Fields is peddling a screenplay to Esoteric Studios producer Franklin Pangborn. As he enters the studio, he stands in front of a large poster heralding *The Bank Dick* with a picture of Fields, but no one walking by recognizes him. Fields reads a scene to Pangborn, then the movie cuts to the scene itself, in near-blackout style. The effect is confusing, to say the least; audiences could only be disoriented at seeing Margaret Dumont as a mountain-dwelling Amazon named Mrs. Hemogloben, equipped with a tiara, guard dogs, and a daughter called Ouliotta (Susan Miller) in one scene, and then being shunted back to the story conference with Pangborn in the next.

The "plot" Fields proposes is pure madness: on his way with his niece to Mexico to make a fortune selling nutmegs, Fields falls out of an airplane trying to retrieve a bottle of booze which has dropped out of the window. He winds up in a mountaintop Russian colony, where he meets Miss Dumont, toys with her daughter, but finally decides that he'd better stay with the mother since she has the money. The

NEVER GIVE A SUCKER AN EVEN BREAK (1941). With Margaret Dumont

NEVER GIVE A SUCKER AN EVEN BREAK (1941). With Jody Gilbert

characters wear exotic costumes and drink such wild concoctions as spiked goat's milk. Interspersed with the dialogue are some songs, chirped operetta-style by Fields' niece, Gloria Jean.

The upshot is that Pangborn fires Fields for thinking up such a far-out script in the first place, and the "real" movie ends with a masterful chase sequence resembling, but better than, the chase in *The Bank Dick*. In commenting on the film, critic Otis Ferguson said: "There is nobody who makes bad comedies more funny than Fields—who is responsible for making them bad in the first place."

And, of course, it's true: whether he's having a run-in with Jody Gilbert, a buxom greasy-spoon waitress whom he addresses as "Blimpie Pie" as she spills water on him ("There's no extra charge for the cold shower, I hope," he remarks); or responding to his secretary's warning that "someday you'll drown in a vat of whiskey," with "Drown in a vat of whiskey? Death, where is thy sting?"; or falling off a 2,000-foot cliff and commenting, "It's the last foot that's dangerous," Fields' unique, almost nonchalant combination of slapstick and burlesque sparkles throughout.

Piling insanity upon insanity, Fields even sings a song about "chickens having pretty legs" as the camera cuts to shots of pretty women. (Nobody ever accused Fields of *not* being a male chauvinist.) The irony of the Fields persona is that audiences knew full well that he was putting them on, but at the same time they knew that he was being himself, openly and honestly. For instance, he does a scene in a soda fountain which was obviously supposed to be a saloon, and remarks directly to the audience: "This scene's supposed to be a saloon, but the censor cut it out. It'll play just as well."

Never Give a Sucker an Even Break is probably the most ramshackle of the four Universal films, but its ineptitude only further strengthened the legions of Fields' fans who delighted in his elevation of the art of slapstick to a state of fundamental anarchy, while systematically managing to milk every chaotic moment for the most laughs.

In 1939 there appeared a book written by Fields called *Fields for President*. In the main, it was compiled from various articles, notes and jottings that he had worked on from time to time during his career. In the book he commented on or lambasted practically everything that had irked him during the years and set the record straight on many subjects, including marriage (he thought the institution was "a crutch for the weak"); political campaigns (he insisted that political baby-kissing come to an end); income tax ("the major responsibility of a President is to squeeze the last possible cent out of the taxpayer"); the rules of etiquette (he disapproved of most social amenities); physical fitness (he enjoyed tennis and golf and had a mechanical rowing machine installed in his home); babies (he didn't like them); and business (he thought that, at the very least, a good president should know how to run a business successfully). All in all, the book is a delight and probably contains more common-sense advice, page for page, than most legitimate party campaign primers.

After *Never Give a Sucker an Even Break,* Fields' last film for Universal, he made *Tales of Manhattan* (1942) for 20th Century-Fox. He was now seriously ill, and could not take the strain—nor would the studios take the risk—of his making another feature film. The movie was a series of unrelated stories showcasing a number of stars (including Charles Boyer, Rita Hayworth, Ginger Rogers, Henry Fonda, Edward G. Robinson and others), linked together by the passing of a tuxedo from person to person. Unfortunately, Fields' segment, co-starring Margaret Dumont, was cut (to reduce the overall running time) before the picture was released to exhibitors, and has never been publicly shown to this day.

Fields' remaining three films were made in 1944 and were basically "guest" appearances. Directed by Fields' old friend Edward Sutherland, *Follow the Boys* (Universal) was a typical wartime musical salute to American fighting men, starring George Raft and Vera Zorina, and featuring guest appearances by Fields, Orson Welles, Marlene Dietrich, and Jeanette MacDonald, among others. Fields does his by-now-celebrated poolhall routine, and spices his appearance with a brief juggling act. He seems well enough, although the strain of his continuing illness is revealed in candid, unretouched stills

117

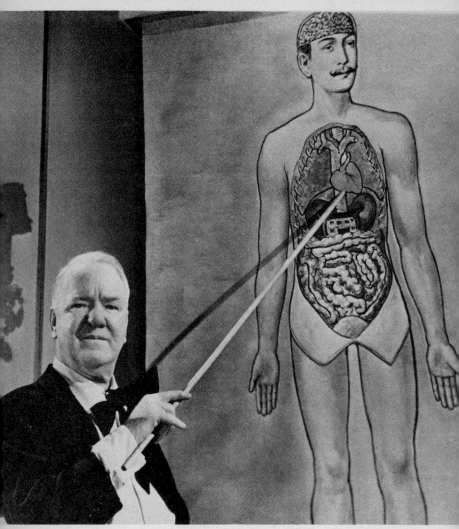

TALES OF MANHATTAN (1942). Fields gives an anatomy lesson, in the episode dropped from the film.

FOLLOW THE BOYS (1944). With Bill Wolf

taken of him on the set. It is said that he was overcome by insomnia during this last period and would often drive around Hollywood in his huge car with Miss Monti, looking at the pedestrians.

Fields' next-to-last film was *Song of the Open Road* (United Artists), a musical created to launch a young singer, Jane Powell. It is ironic that this newly discovered child star (she was then fourteen) made her first movie with a man whom the public believed to be a child-hating comedian. She recently remarked: "That was long before W.C. Fields became a legend. I wish I knew he was going to be such a legend, I could have dined out the rest of my life on those stories. As for his hating kids, he was always very polite with me."

In the film. Miss Powell plays, with girlish charm, a runaway film star who, with more good will than experience, joins a group of government fruit-pickers. The film's climax calls for a rousing Hollywood show (featuring stints by Fields and Edgar Bergen and Charlie McCarthy). It was an all-too-brief and unmemorable appearance for Fields, although he did spice up the proceedings with a few good laughs.

In 1944, Fields, at sixty-five, made his final film, *Sensations of 1945* (United Artists), directed by Andrew Stone and starring Eleanor Powell. Thankfully, he had a bit more to do than in his preceding film, and his guest appearance was a welcome sight for audiences. Turned out in a twenties fur coat and straw hat, Fields did a mildly amusing comedy skit with a pretty girl in a railway coach (a familiar locale for several of Fields' previous films), but the dialogue was unfunny and aimless. Fields was clearly tired and quite ill—much too ill to perform any of his classic routines which would have required fine timing and a good deal of dexterity.

There were no further movie offers, and Fields, attended by his longtime friend and companion, Carlotta Monti, and others who visited him daily, remained at his rented home on DeMille Drive until he finally had to leave there for a sanitarium. His friend Gene Fowler has said that, to the end. Fields was a man so perversely proud that he preferred to have his friends think him a bit tipsy when, in truth, he was actually gravely ill.* His liver ailment, weakened heart and assorted other maladies intensified, and death (which he referred to as "the Man in the Bright Night-

*At one time, he jokingly observed that the hospital knew he had passed a crisis when they found him "blowing the foam from his medicine."

SONG OF THE OPEN ROAD (1944).
With Edgar Bergen

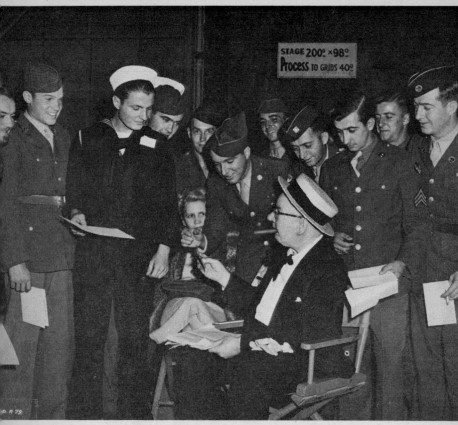

In 1943, Fields signs autographs for servicemen.

gown") came on Christmas Day in 1946. It is said that his final words were lines recited verbatim from Dickens—the Mr. Micawber character—and that just before he died he opened his eyes and winked.

Even near death, Fields had a refreshing enough perspective on life to laugh at it. He bequeathed two fly-catchers and two bottles of Shalimar perfume to Carlotta Monti (whom he referred to endearingly as "Chinaman"). She also received fifty dollars a week for ten years plus Fields' 1938 sixteen-cylinder Cadillac. But the major portion of the Fields fortune went to his estranged wife and her son Claude, who were awarded a substantial amount of the $800,000 estate in court. Fields had expressly stated that he wanted his fortune to be used for the establishment of the "W.C. Fields College for Orphan White Boys and Girls, Where No Religion of Any Sort Is to Be Preached." His will was not followed.

On December 27th of that year, a full-page ad in *The Hollywood Reporter* placed by his friends, read:

The most prejudiced and honest and beloved figure of our so-called "Colony" went away on a day that he pretended to abhor—"Christmas." We loved him, and—peculiarly enough—he loved us. To the most authentic humorist since Mark Twain, to the greatest heart that has beaten since the Middle Ages—W.C. Fields, our friend.

A CRITICAL APPRAISAL: WHY AUDIENCES REACT

Comedy is very difficult to film, and Fields especially has often been referred to as an "anti-film comedian." Everything in film comedy should be spare, quick and precise, but these are not necessarily the elements which directors are first to seize upon in shaping their films. That is why the best of Fields' movies are those which he himself has shaped, as he aims his comedy directly at behavioral patterns rather than relying on cinematic effects. How often, if ever, have we been distracted by elaborate tracking shots, artful lighting or sophisticated editing techniques in a Fields film? The answer is not very often, and that is as it should be.

By most critical standards, Fields' pictures are not very well put together and often show as much contempt for the narrative line as they do for most everything else. Critic James Agee often complained of the lack of even a modicum of direction in Fields' films (but how else can we describe the kind of authority which he exercised over many of his roles?), and critic Otis Ferguson once said that Fields "moved mountains until they fell on him, and then he brushed himself off and looked around for more."

Fields does not work so hard at being irreverent, daring or iconoclastic that you feel exhausted just watching so much sound, fury and bluster. On the other hand, his harangues overflow with unexpected truths, as he manages to satirize cleverly just about everything and everybody with whom he comes into contact. The definitive Fieldsian character role represents an observation of ordinary people caught in life's funny sadness and trapped in its ultimate irony.

His brand of humor is bitter, often uncomfortable, and sometimes even destructive. But whether his mind was in need of an "overhaul, or dry cleaning," as comedian-director Woody Allen has suggested, is debatable. What is *not* debatable is that Fields was probably America's patron saint of "going too far," just as writer-director Mel Brooks probably fills that role today. His films were almost always awesomely funny, yet many people were bound to despise them—and Fields expected, even counted on, this reaction. Whether or not Fields was the forerunner of the kind of *Mad Magazine* humor of the sixties, he *was* a primitive—an artist who specialized in the humor of affront just as comedian Don

MY LITTLE CHICKADEE (1940). With George Moran

NEVER GIVE A SUCKER AN EVEN BREAK (1941). Fields offers his friend a drink.

Rickles does today. Even though most of today's generation is overjoyed by Fields' constant put-downs, his movie-joke insults to so-called civilized sensibilities, good taste and common sense probably made it difficult if not impossible for his contemporary critics to place an objective value on his genius.

Most of Fields' films are neither sturdy nor beguiling; their emotional appeal lies in their skillful ability to convulse audiences by reducing almost all values to mere confetti. Fields' brand of humor has its emotional heart deep in his own neuroses. From all accounts of his life, it's clear that he genuinely suffered as a child, and even later in life; but he also knew how to *use* his anxiety/paranoia, to convert his well-known and highly publicized fears and even hates toward certain institutions and objects into an ultimate filmic resolution, as if in doing so the process purged him of deleterious feelings. Many of his characters go through a chaotic stage and wind up with their situation ultimately salvaged, if not improved. Like their creator, these Fieldsian protagonists know how to dramatize their feelings. In its best moments, Fields' Theater-of-the-Absurd approach to movies presents us head-on with the irrationality and the illogicality of most human experience. The Fantastic and The Nonsensical have, after all, (e.g. Chaplin and Keaton) a rather long and respected tradition in movies. Fields' special quality of refinement is that, having rejected almost all traditional notions of plot and character, he ends up dramatizing his themes quite extensively through language. More so than with most screen comedians, many of the impossibilities and improbabilities of a Fields film are carried out not by what we see, but by what we hear.

In fact, there is some reason to believe that what we hear remains at such a distance from what we see, that on film Fieldsian language nearly breaks loose from its total context and begins to assume a completely independent existence. This probably did not happen with his theater performances, since by the very nature of the theater, audiences instinctively adopt a certain "artificial" sense from the moment the curtain rises. On film, however, when language is not translated one-to-one into visual terms, the very nature of the words themselves may tend not only to contradict, but to overwhelm the pictures themselves. Most movie audiences today have been conditioned by television, so that viewers always want to *hear* comedy even if they don't always concentrate on *looking at* it. This is why most Fields films play very well on television.

TILLIE AND GUS (1933). Fields and Alison Skipworth in trouble.

Fields himself has said of comedy:

> The funniest thing about comedy is that you never know why people laugh. I know *what* makes them laugh, but trying to get your hands on the *why* of it is like trying to pick an eel out of a tub of water . . . You usually can't get a laugh out of damaging anything valuable. When you kick a silk hat, it must be dilapidated; when you wreck a car, bang it up a little before you bring it on the scene . . . I know we laugh at the troubles of others, provided those troubles are not too serious . . . The reason some folks don't laugh at most gags is that their first emotional reaction is to feel sorry for people instead of to laugh at them.*

One of the most striking features of many Fields films is the frequent incoherence, even downright inaudibility, of the dialogue. The fact is that in context it may even seem somewhat senseless, pointless or absurd. Contributing to this effect is Fields' monotonous nasal delivery, usually emotionless and sour. This is not to say that what we are shown on the screen is less interesting or challenging than what we hear on the soundtrack, as is sometimes the case with film comedians such as Jacques Tati. Nevertheless, to a greater extent than with either

Chaplin or Keaton, we find ourselves intensely listening to Fields' films rather than merely watching them—as we would watch a Laurel and Hardy movie, for example. The marvelous manner in which Fields intensifies our sense of language by shrinking it into a strange and disembodied state of conversation is unique in film comedy.

Most Fields films are screen comedies turned upside down and inside out, braced with a lot of low burlesque. However, unlike certain comedies which make a desperate attempt to win over the viewer, Fields' films exhibit no strain—there's an ease of style about them which does not exhaust the audience. If anything, it makes the viewer want the film to be even funnier and more intense than he remembers, and the satisfaction of watching a Fields character stumble through to usually unearned (but not necessarily undeserved) riches is a marvelous experience for any audience—especially the Ordinary Man.

Viewing a Fields film is not as tiring an experience as, say, viewing a Keaton or Langdon film. When Fields is being insulting or rude, knocking down sacred cows like clay pigeons, or when he goes "too far," his comedy has a rewarding shock effect. That is because his style and vision have a specific center of gravity, and although his

*W.C. Fields, "Anything for a Laugh." September 1934, in Donald Decshner's, *The Films of W.C. Fields* (The Citadel Press, New Jersey: 1972), pp. 29-32.

THE BANK DICK (1940). Fields and his loving family

films sometimes escape the consciousness of those with short attention spans, Fields appreciates the need for getting a joke to his audience fast and then moving on. He builds momentum and audience sympathy through his continuimg characters, and even though everything around him seems slapdash and chaotic, his own comedy is a wonder of anarchic discipline.

As an actor, Fields was no chameleon—he could not totally transform himself on-screen like Laurence Olivier or Alec Guinness. From part to part, Fields' face and voice, his gestures and walk remain essentially the same. Because of this, a distinctive and, for some, distracting, persona would hover over Fields' various characterizations. This does not mean that Fields, as an actor, was less versatile than those who are chameleon-like; rather, that by the very nature of his physique, voice, mannerisms, personality and total character, Fields soon became a sharply defined presence to audiences. They knew what to expect of Fields and of his variations on a theme. They expected and wanted Fields to tailor roles to his own personality, and then cleverly embellish them out of his comedian's grab-bag of surface effects.

Fields' versatility as an actor is due to the fact that, while not necessarily aspiring to versatility, he could articulate subtle variations of the same suffering middle-class character *because* filmgoers kept wanting to revisit that particular persona and to keep accepting it. They did not want any deeply felt characterizations to obscure the essential truths. Fields' popularity was based on his commitment to the strong screen personality—one who retains from film to film a consistent set of qualities and a specific comic identity. Those periods when Fields fell out of favor with either audiences or critics resulted more from the audience's and the critics' change in taste and types than from any change in Fields.

He would probably have thought that movie comedy was really not much fun to write about since it should be as obvious as the nose on one's face (no pun intended). And he would have been correct. Fields preferred not writing *about* comedy, but simply writing comedy itself. His words reflect his bigotries—a pure uncomplicated variety—untarnished by dogma. Fields neither wants nor appeals for love, compassion, justice, or poignancy; his nihilistic strain is first cousin to that of the Marx Brothers (although Fields' delivery was slow and drawn-out, while the Marx Brothers style was rat-tat-tat, hurly-burly fast). Fields would have probably liked Lenny Bruce's wit, although the two comedians differ

NEVER GIVE A SUCKER AN EVEN BREAK (1941). Fields confronts an unaccustomed beverage: an ice cream soda.

in that Fields took care to give his audiences some clues here and there as to his fundamental decency and honorable intentions.

As to whether Fields was primarily a "man's comedian," it seems fairly safe to estimate that female audiences generally found him immensely repugnant—a "dirty old man," no less. Yet those with fairly strong stomachs and a good eye and ear for the satanic style might have had second thoughts. By and large, However, the bulk of Fields' loyal followers were men who probably considered him no more or less than they would another drinking buddy. They would have genuinely felt comfortable with him in the poolroom or the barroom.

As a group, men certainly identified more readily with Fields than with Chaplin or Keaton, both of whom displayed a certain coquettish style which women often thought attractive. Fields was a man's man—a fighter, but not a lover; a cheater, but not a loser. If he had had any sex appeal, he might have attracted the same kind of audiences that identified with James Cagney. But rather than sex appeal, Fields will be most remembered for his memorable one-liners, his verbal equivalents of Cagney's grapefruit-in-the-face.

Fields' basic physical vocabulary consisted of pantomime, mugging, double entendre and, to some extent, deadpan—plus a hefty dose of insult. His use of props was generally limited to such trusted longtime items as a cane, a straw hat, a set of golf clubs, or anything else he might get his juggling hands on. Fields is less a lovable eccentric than he is a universal reflector of life's petty harassments, and if we had Fields around today, he would probably systematically destroy most causes, crusades, myths and anti-heroes. The mind boggles at how Fields might attack such subjects as Women's Lib, Watergate or the new Sexual Liberation in movies. Fields' free-form attacks on the American middle-class pieties, the bricks he threw at the establishment when that sort of behavior, especially by a "movie star," was not considered good form, would be applauded today. In fact, it is.

THE PRIVATE LIFE STYLE AND THE PUBLIC PERSONALITY

In his 1953 book *Broadway Heartbeat*, Bernard Sobel reflected on Fields: "Hollywood made Fields an autocrat whose odd behavior was matched only by his drinking prowess. Somehow I can't believe that he let fame distort him." And, of course, he didn't let fame distort him, although it gave him a greater amount of time and money to expand on some of his "vices."

During his vaudeville days, Fields was known for traveling with three trunks—one containing clothes, two containing liquor, and he offered this advice to fellow travelers: "Always carry a flagon of whiskey in case of snakebite, and furthermore always carry a small snake."

It was probably on his first European tour that Fields discovered, in English public houses, the sedative effects of hard liquor. Until that time, he had indulged mainly in beer (from childhood) and champagne (after he began earning a decent salary). Pubs brought out his fondness for Irish whiskey, and in later years he would switch almost exclusively to martinis—long on the gin and short on the vermouth. In his drinking prime, he put away two quarts of liquor every day.

Yet most of his close friends agreed that Fields never appeared drunk. Edgar Bergen once said: "Fields could be drinking in the morning, drinking and drinking in the afternoon. But he never acted as if he were drunk."

Once, while on tour together, Will Rogers said to Fields: "Bill, aren't you worried? Don't you know that those martinis are *slow* poison?" And Fields answered: "I'm in no hurry, son."

During his last illness, doctors warned Fields that he'd lose his hearing if he continued to drink. But he had an answer for that: "I don't think I will. The stuff I've been drinking is so much better than the stuff I've been hearing." It was to his credit, though, that Fields never wanted or liked to be thought of as a drunkard, only as a man who had a very great capacity for drink.

Of course, Fields' best answer to those who called him drunk was an answer he gave to a disapproving critic in *It's a Gift:* "I'm drunk and you're crazy. But I'll be sober tomorrow and you'll be crazy for the rest of your life."

During this period, and for most of his professional life, Fields was attended by a small group of

YOU CAN'T CHEAT AN HONEST MAN (1939). With Charlie McCarthy and Edgar Bergen

At a Masquers party celebrating Fields' forty years in show business:
Leslie Howard, Fred MacMurray, and George Arliss

MY LITTLE CHICKADEE (1940). Fields and Mae West take the plunge, while Margaret Hamilton looks on.

friends—almost exclusively men— who found his odd, offbeat personality somehow endearing. (Of course Miss Monti and Fields' longtime devoted secretary Magda Michael were exceptions to this male bastion of intimates.) They stuck by him to the end because of a basic and continuing affection, although he constantly baited and trapped them, probably to test their friendship. Their curiosity, in not knowing what he would do next, may have kept them in tow.

"Uncle Claude," as he was known by them, was described by his friend Gene Fowler as follows: "He was the most ornery lovable man I have ever known. He hid none of his faults from the world, indeed he hid nothing except perhaps some of his money, and most of his good deeds, which were more numerous than might be imagined."*

Fields' delight in using strange phrases and outrageous names for his movie characters and as pseudonyms for his screenplays is well known—almost as well known as his strong dislike for his home town, Philadelphia. In *My Little Chickadee*, a posse which is about to hang him asks Fields if he has one last request. He answers: "Yes, I'd like to see Paris before I die." But as the noose tightens, he concedes,

*Gene Fowler, *Minutes of the Last Meeting* The Viking Press, New York: 1954, p. 106.

"Philadelphia will do!" An interviewer once asked him in the thirties what he would like on his epitaph. Fields, finding the subject sufficiently bizarre to be interesting, responded: "On the whole I'd rather be in Philadelphia."

Like Dickens, Fields adored peculiar words and names. Many of these would weave in and out of his on and off-screen conversations: jobbernowl, posy, smidgen, modest repast and, of course, "Godfrey Daniel," "Mother-of-Pearl," "Suffering Sciatica," and "Drat!" Among his characters' names were: Chester Snavely, Ouliotta Hemogloben, Egbert Sousé, A. Pismo Clam, Ampico J. Steinway and Father Favania. His pseudonyms were equally outrageous, including such ear-busters as Otis Criblecoblis, Charles Bogle and Mahatma Kane Jeeves.

Although Fields is commonly believed to have had a low attitude toward all children (his jealousy of Baby LeRoy is well documented), nevertheless he wished a large part of his fortune to be willed for an orphans' home, and he even deliberately wrote Baby LeRoy into a film when the child's option came due to ensure that the studio would continue to employ him.

In this and many other ways, Fields' life is full of contradictions. He once said, "Never try to impress a woman, because if you do she'll

138

NEVER GIVE A SUCKER AN EVEN BREAK (1941). With Leon Errol

Relaxing on the set

expect you to keep up to the standard for the rest of your life. And the pace, my friends, is devastating." Yet the facts speak otherwise with regard to his feminine liaisons.

But what is most interesting about Fields' private life style and public personality is that there appears to be a strong consistency between both. The same paranoid fears and notions that many of his screen characters displayed (and a good number of them were largely written by Fields himself) are seen in his private lifestyle. Some of the enjoyment in looking back on Fields' life and films is in trying to delineate the mystery of the exact relationship of art and life in his work. From most evidence, it appears that he was much the same off and on stage and screen.

His drinking, his distrust of doctors (he once said, "When doctors and undertakers meet, they always wink at each other") and lawyers, his belief in the basic unfairness of the law, his low regard for most women, children, dogs, servants and governments in power, plus his satisfaction at having a good deal of cash on hand to forestall any "lean years"—all of these turn up in his films. Even picnics, which Fields loved to organize, appear in some of the more charming sequences in his movies. (One recalls the lovely picnic sequence in *It's a Gift* as the Bissonette family is

traveling west.)

In a word, when Fields worked out his own aggressions on film, audiences also worked out theirs—*with* Fields. His most effective weapon was satire, and he used it to take revenge on those people and institutions which caused him the most grief during his vulnerable years. Fields was an original—some have even put forth the thesis that his humor has a startlingly surrealistic touch about it—because his very identity was his own best publicity. Even today, we hear commercials using a voice obviously modeled after Fields, urging prospective customers to buy draft beer ("because when you have a can around, you don't need a woman, but it certainly doesn't hurt to have one"), and prunes. (A Fields-like drawling voice says, "I had to beat the little pest down with my cane to keep him away from the jar of prunes.") These attest to his continuing power and identification for the public—almost thirty years after his death.

Fields is that rarity—a verbal comedian who also knew how to use his body and when to allow his unconscious to take over. He is not a universal fellow like Chaplin, nor physically as graceful as Keaton, but we enjoy his performances because his essential sanity comes through in the end. His films, for the most part, are disorganized

The Great Man in a reflective mood

and somewhat messy, his plots tend to evaporate right before our eyes, and most characters around him are not strong enough to compete with his presence. But Fields knew *how* to trust audiences, and that has been his success, for when he is battered and scarred and threatened, so are we, too; but when he goes all the way to success, so do we, too.

His films never really impose themselves on our consciousness—his essential comedy is, in fact, mysterious because it tends to dissolve and even merge into the same routine in our memory again and again. But we enjoy his familiar show—no matter how often, because W.C. Fields up there on-screen is essentially a very real person. His malice and irreverence would probably elevate him to the status of true hero if he were making pictures today. Fields' power lies in his ability to dramatize man's preposterous deviations from what is considered the norm. But, unlike Chaplin, he does not comment directly on the world's "insanity"; rather, he greets it defenselessly and head-on. He may have offered audiences little comfort in his day by letting the chips fall where they may, but watching his films today, with the perspective of history, is not only a comfort but a joy.

BIBLIOGRAPHY

Agee, James. *Agee on Film*. Beacon Press, Boston, 1958.

Anobile, Richard J. *A Flask Of Fields*. W.W. Norton and Company, Inc., New York, 1972.

Bergman, Andrew. *We're In the Money*. New York University Press, New York, 1971.

Brooks, Louise. "The Other Face of W.C. Fields," *Sight and Sound*, Spring, 1971.

Cantor, Eddie. *As I Remember Them*. Duell, Sloan, and Pearce. New York, 1963.

Deschner, Donald. *The Films of W.C. Fields*. Citadel Press, New York, 1966.

Everson, William K. *The Art of W.C. Fields*. Bobbs-Merrill, Co., New York, 1967.

Ferguson, Otis. *Collected Film Criticism*. Temple University Press, Philadelphia, 1971.

Fields, Ronald J. *W.C. Fields By Himself: His Intended Autobiography*. Prentice-Hall, Inc., Englewood Cliffs, N.J., 1973.

Fields, W.C. *Drat! Being the Encapsulated View of Life, In His Own Words*. World Publishing Company, New York, 1968.

Fields, W.C. *Fields For President*. Dell Publishing Co., Inc., New York, 1972.

Fields, W.C. "From Boy Juggler To Star Comedian," *Theatre Magazine*, New York, October, 1928.

Fields, W.C. *I Never Met a Kid I Liked*. Stanyan Books, Los Angeles, 1970.

Fowler, Gene. *Minutes of the Last Meeting*. The Viking Press, New York, 1954.

Gilbert, Douglas. *American Vaudeville: Its Life and Times*. Dover Publications, Inc., New York, 1963.

Greene, Grahame. *Grahame Greene On Film*. Simon and Schuster, New York, 1972.

Markfield, Wallace. "Dark Geography of W.C. Fields," *New York Times Magazine*. April 24, 1966.

Mast, Gerald. *The Comic Mind: Comedy and the Movies*. The Bobbs-Merrill Company, Inc. New York, 1973.

Monti, Carlotta. *W.C. Fields and Me*. Prentice-Hall, Inc., Englewood Cliffs, N.J. 1971.

Robinson, David. "Dukenfield meets McGargle," *Sight and Sound*, Summer, 1967.

Sobel, Bernard. *Broadway Heartbeat*. Hermitage House, New York, 1953.

Taylor, Robert Lewis. *W.C. Fields: His Follies and Fortunes*. New American Library, New York, 1967.

Tibbles, Percy Thomas. *The Magician's Handbook*. Dawbarn and Ward, Ltd., London, 1901.

Tynan, Kenneth. *Curtains*. Lowe and Brydone, Ltd. London, 1961.

THE FILMS OF W.C. FIELDS

The director's name follows the release date. Sp indicates screenplay and b/o indicates based on.

1. POOL SHARKS. The Gaumont Company, 1915. *Edwin Middleton*. One-reeler, with Fields repeating his famous pool game routine.

2. HIS LORDSHIP'S DILEMMA. The Mutual Company, 1915. *William Haddock*. One-reeler. No prints are known to exist today.

3. JANICE MEREDITH. MGM, 1925. *E. Mason Hopper*. Sp: Lillie Hayward, b/o novel by Paul Leicester. Cast: Marion Davies, Harrison Ford, Macklyn Arbuckle, Joseph Kilgour, Tyrone Power, Sr. No complete print exists today.

4. SALLY OF THE SAWDUST. United Artists, 1925. *D.W. Griffith*. Sp: Forrest Halsey, b/o stage play *Poppy* by Dorothy Donnelly. Cast: Carol Dempster, Alfred Lunt, Erville Alderson, Effie Shannon, Charles Hammond, Roy Applegate. Fields repeats his stage role. Remade as *Poppy* in 1936.

5. THAT ROYLE GIRL. Paramount, 1926. *D.W. Griffith*. Sp: Paul Schofield, b/o story by Edwin Balmer. Cast: Carol Dempster, James Kirkwood, Harrison Ford, Paul Everton, Kathleen Chambers. No known prints exist today.

6. IT'S THE OLD ARMY GAME. Paramount, 1926. *Edward Sutherland*. Sp: Thomas J. Geraghty, b/o play by J.P. McEvoy. Cast: Louise Brooks, Blanche Ring, William Gaxton, Mary Foy, Mickey Bennett. Remade as *It's a Gift* in 1934.

7. SO'S YOUR OLD MAN. Famous Players-Lasky Corp., 1926. *Gregory La Cava*. Sp: J. Clarkson Miller, b/o adaptation by Howard Emmett Rogers of *Mr. Brisbee's Princess*, by Julian Street. Cast: Alice Joyce, Charles Rogers, Marcia Harris, Julia Ralph. Remade as *You're Telling Me* in 1934.

8. RUNNING WILD. Paramount, 1927. *Gregory La Cava*. Sp: Roy Briant. Cast: Mary Brian, Claud Buchanan, Marie Shotwell, Barney Raskle, Frederick Burton, J. Moy Bennett, Frank Evans. Remade as *Man on the Flying Trapeze* in 1935.

9. **TWO FLAMING YOUTHS.** Paramount, 1927. *John Waters.* Sp: Percy Heath and Donald Davis, b/o original story by Percy Heath. Cast: Chester Conklin, Mary Brian, Jack Luden, George Irving, Cissy Fitzgerald, Jimmie Quinn. Remade as *The Old-Fashioned Way* in 1934.

10. **THE POTTERS.** Famous Players-Lasky Corp., distributed by Paramount, 1927. *Fred Newmeyer.* Sp: J. Clarkson Miller, b/o J.P. McEvoy's play of the same name. Cast: Mary Alden, Ivy Harris, Jack Egan, "Skeets" Gallagher, Joseph Smiley, Bradley Barker. No known prints available today.

11. **TILLIE'S PUNCTURED ROMANCE.** Paramount, 1928. *Edward Sutherland.* Sp: Monte Brice and Keene Thompson, b/o characters from earlier film of the same title. Cast: Louise Fazenda, Chester Conklin, Mack Swain, Doris Hill, Grant Withers, Tom Kennedy, Babe London, Billy Platt.

12. **FOOLS FOR LUCK.** Paramount, 1928. *Charles F. Reisner.* Sp: J. Walter Ruben. Cast: Chester Conklin, Sally Blane, Jack Luden, Mary Alden, Arthur Housman, Robert Dudley, Martha Mattox.

13. **THE GOLF SPECIALIST.** RKO, 1930. *Monte Brice.* Sp: W.C. Fields. Fields' first sound film, a two-reeler.

14. **HER MAJESTY, LOVE.** Warner Bros. 1931. *William Dieterle.* Sp: Robert Lord and Arthur Caesar, b/o original story by R. Berbrauer and R. Oesterreicher. Cast: Marilyn Miller, Ben Lyon, Ford Sterling, Leon Errol, Chester Conklin, Maude Eburne, Fields' first feature-length sound film.

15. **THE DENTIST.** Paramount/Mack Sennett, 1932. *Leslie Pearce.* Sp: W.C. Fields. Cast: Babe Kane. First of four Sennett two-reelers.

16. **IF I HAD A MILLION.** Paramount, 1932. *Ernst Lubitsch, Norman Taurog, Stephen Roberts, Norman McLeod, James Cruze, William A. Seiter, H. Bruce Humberstone.* Sp: Claude Binyon, Whitney Bolton, Sidney Buchman, Joseph L. Mankiewicz, Seton I. Miller, and thirteen others. Cast: Gary Cooper, George Raft, Charles Laughton, Jack Oakie, Charlie Ruggles, Alison Skipworth, Mary Boland. Multi-segment film, with Fields and Skipworth in slapstick auto-wrecking sequence.

17. **MILLION DOLLAR LEGS.** Paramount, 1932. *Edward Cline.* Sp: Henry Myers and Nick Barrows, b/o story by Joseph L. Mankiewicz. Cast: Jack Oakie, Andy Clyde, Lydia Roberti, Susan Fleming, Ben Turpin, Hugh Herbert, George Barbier.

18. **THE BARBER SHOP.** Paramount/Mack Sennett, 1933. *Arthur Ripley*. Sp: W.C. Fields. Cast: Elise Cavanna, Harry Watson, Dagmar Oakland. Sennett two-reeler.

19. **THE FATAL GLASS OF BEER.** Paramount/Mack Sennett, 1933. *Clyde Bruckman*. Sp: W.C. Fields. Cast: Rosemary Theby, George Chandler, Richard Cramer. Sennett two-reeler.

20. **THE PHARMACIST.** Paramount/Mack Sennett, 1933. *Arthur Ripley*. Sp: W.C. Fields. Cast: Babe Kane, Elise Cavanna, Grady Sutton, Lorena Carr. Sennett two-reeler.

21. **INTERNATIONAL HOUSE.** Paramount, 1933. *Edward Sutherland*. Sp: Francis Martin and Walter DeLeon, b/o story by Lou Heifetz and Neil Brant. Cast: Peggy Hopkins Joyce, Stuart Erwin, Sari Maritza, George Burns, Gracie Allen, Bela Lugosi, Edmund Breese, Lumsden Hare, Franklin Pangborn.

22. **ALICE IN WONDERLAND.** Paramount, 1933. *Norman McLeod*. Sp: Joseph L. Mankiewicz and William Cameron Menzies, b/o book by Lewis Carroll. Cast: Charlotte Henry, Richard Arlen, Gary Cooper, Leon Errol, Louise Fazenda, Cary Grant, Sterling Holloway, Edward Everett Horton, Baby LeRoy, Mae Marsh, Edna May Oliver, Charlie Ruggles, Alison Skipworth. Fields as Humpty-Dumpty.

23. **TILLIE AND GUS.** Paramount, 1933. *Francis Martin*. Sp: Walter DeLeon and Francis Martin, b/o story by Rupert Hughes. Cast: Alison Skipworth, Baby LeRoy, Jacqueline Wells, Clifford Jones, Clarence Wilson, George Barbier, Barton MacLane, Edgar Kennedy.

24. **SIX OF A KIND.** Paramount, 1934. *Leo McCarey*. Sp: Walter DeLeon and Harry Ruskin, b/o original story by Keene Thompson and Douglas MacLean. Cast: Charlie Ruggles, Mary Boland, George Burns, Gracie Allen, Alison Skipworth, Bradley Page, Grace Bradley, James Burke.

25. **YOU'RE TELLING ME.** Paramount, 1934. *Erle Kenton*. Sp: Walter DeLeon and Paul M. Jones, b/o story by Julian Street. Cast: Joan Marsh, Larry "Buster" Crabbe, Adrienne Ames, Louise Carter, Kathleen Howard, James B. Kenton, Robert McKenzie. Remake of *So's Your Old Man*.

26. **MRS. WIGGS OF THE CABBAGE PATCH.** Paramount, 1934. *Norman Taurog*. Sp: William Slavens McNutt and Jane Storm, b/o novel and play by Alice Hegan Rice and Anne Crawford Flexner. Cast: Pauline Lord, ZaSu Pitts, Evelyn Venable, Kent Taylor, Charles Middleton, Donald Meek, Jimmy Butler. Previously filmed in 1914 and 1919 and remade in 1942.

27. IT'S A GIFT. Paramount, 1934. *Norman Taurog*. Sp: Jack Cunningham, b/o original story by Charles Bogle (W.C. Fields) and J.P. McEvoy. Cast: Jean Rouverol, Julian Madison, Kathleen Howard, Tom Bupp, Tammany Young, Baby LeRoy, Morgan Wallace, Charles Sellon. Remake of *It's the Old Army Game*.

28. THE OLD-FASHIONED WAY. Paramount, 1934. *William Beaudine*. Sp: Garnett Weston and Jack Cunningham, b/o original story by Charles Bogle (W.C. Fields). Cast: Joe Morrison, Judith Allen, Jan Duggan, Nora Cecil, Baby LeRoy, Jack Mulhall. Remake of *Two Flaming Youths*.

29. MISSISSIPPI. Paramount, 1935. *Edward Sutherland*. Sp: Francis Martin and Jack Cunningham, as adapted by Herbert Fields and Claude Binyon from story by Booth Tarkington. Cast: Bing Crosby, Joan Bennett, Queenie Smith, Gail Patrick, Claude Gillingwater, John Miljan, Edward Pawley.

30. MAN ON THE FLYING TRAPEZE. Paramount, 1935. *Clyde Bruckman*. Sp: Ray Harris, Sam Hardy, Jack Cunningham, Bobby Vernon, b/o original story by Charles Bogle (W.C. Fields). Cast: Mary Brian, Kathleen Howard, Grady Sutton, Vera Lewis, Lucien Littlefield, Oscar Apfel, Lew Kelly, Walter Brennan. Remake of *Running Wild*.

31. DAVID COPPERFIELD. MGM, 1935. *George Cukor*. Sp: Howard Estabrook, b/o novel by Charles Dickens. Cast: Lionel Barrymore, Maureen O'Sullivan, Madge Evans, Edna May Oliver, Lewis Stone, Freddie Bartholomew, Frank Lawton, Elizabeth Allan, Roland Young, Basil Rathbone, Elsa Lanchester.

32. POPPY. Paramount, 1936. *Edward Sutherland*. Sp: Waldemar Young and Virginia Van Upp, b/o play by Dorothy Donnelly. Cast: Rochelle Hudson, Richard Cromwell, Granville Bates, Catharine Doucet, Lynne Overman, Maude Eburne, Rosalind Keith. Remake of *Sally of the Sawdust*.

33. THE BIG BROADCAST OF 1938. Paramount, 1938. *Mitchell Leisen*. Sp: Walter DeLeon, Francis Martin, Ken Englund, b/o original story by Frederick Hazlitt Brennan. Cast: Martha Raye, Dorothy Lamour, Shirley Ross, Lynne Overman, Bob Hope, Ben Blue, Leif Erikson, Grace Bradley.

34. YOU CAN'T CHEAT AN HONEST MAN. Universal, 1939. *George Marshall*. Sp: George Marion, Jr., Richard Mack and Everett Freeman, b/o original story by Charles Bogle (W.C. Fields). Cast: Edgar Bergen, Charlie McCarthy, Mortimer Snerd, Constance Moore, Mary Forbes, Thurston Hall, Eddie Anderson, John Arledge.

35. THE BANK DICK. Universal, 1940. *Edward Cline*. Sp: Mahatma Kane Jeeves (W.C. Fields). Cast: Cora Witherspoon, Una Merkel, Evelyn Del Rio, Jessie Ralph, Franklin Pangborn, Shemp Howard, Richard Purcell, Grady Sutton, Russell Hicks, Pierre Watkin.

36. MY LITTLE CHICKADEE. Universal, 1940. *Edward Cline*. Sp: Mae West and W.C. Fields. Cast: Mae West, Joseph Calleia, Dick Foran, Margaret Hamilton, Donald Meek, Ruth Donnelly.

37. NEVER GIVE A SUCKER AN EVEN BREAK. Universal, 1941. *Edward Cline*. Sp: John T. Neville and Prescott Chaplin, b/o original story by Otis Criblecoblis (W.C. Fields). Cast: Gloria Jean, Anne Nagel, Franklin Pangborn, Mona Barrie, Leon Errol, Margaret Dumont, Susan Miller.

38. TALES OF MANHATTAN. 20th Century-Fox, 1942. *Julien Duvivier*. Sp: Ben Hecht, Ferenc Molnar, Donald Ogden Stewart, Samuel Hoffenstein, Alan Campbell, Ladislas Fodor, L. Vadnai, L. Gorog, Lamar Trotti, Henry Blankfort. Cast: Charles Boyer, Rita Hayworth, Ginger Rogers, Henry Fonda, Charles Laughton, Edward G. Robinson, and many others. Fields' twenty-minute sequence was cut from this film to reduce running time. It has never been restored to film or shown theatrically.

39. FOLLOW THE BOYS. Universal, 1944. *Edward Sutherland*. Sp: Lou Breslow and Gertrude Purcell. Cast: George Raft, Vera Zorina, Charles Grapewin, Grace McDonald, Charles Butterworth, George Macready, Elizabeth Patterson, Regis Toomey. Fields in guest appearance.

40. SONG OF THE OPEN ROAD. United Artists, 1944. *S. Sylvan Simon*. Sp: Albert Mannheimer, b/o unpublished story by Irving Phillips and Edward Verdier. Cast: Charlie McCarthy, Edgar Bergen, Jane Powell, Bonita Granville, Peggy O'Neill, Jackie Moran, Regis Toomey. Fields in guest appearance.

41. SENSATIONS OF 1945. United Artists, 1944. *Andrew L. Stone*. Sp: Dorothy Bennett, b/o original story by Frederick Jackson and Andrew Stone. Cast: Eleanor Powell, Dennis O'Keefe, C. Aubrey Smith, Eugene Pallette, Mimi Forsythe, Lyle Talbot, Sophie Tucker. Fields' swan song in brief guest appearance.

INDEX

ABOUT THE AUTHOR:

Nicholas Yanni has written extensively on movies and television for many publications, including: *The Christian Science Monitor, The Saturday Review, Motion Picture Daily* and *Motion Picture Herald, The Hollywood Reporter, The Independent Film Journal, The Herald, Film Facts, Boxoffice Magazine, The Daily Mirror, Brooklyn Today, HERE In New York* and *The Real Paper*. A Brown graduate, he has taught film courses at Brooklyn College and is completing a Ph.D. in Cinema at New York University where he received a Masters degree in cinema studies. He lives in Greenwich Village.

ABOUT THE EDITOR

Ted Sennett is the author of *Warner Brothers Presents*, a survey of the great Warner films of the Thirties and Forties, and of *Lunatics and Lovers,* on the years of the "screwball" movie comedy. He has also written about films for magazines and newspapers. He lives in New Jersey with his wife and three children.